A Dog Called Perth

A Dog Called Perth

The Voyage of a Beagle

Peter Martin

ORION

The right of Peter Martin to be identified as the author
and illustrator of this work has been asserted by him in
accordance with the Copyright, Designs and Patents
Act 1988.

First published in Great Britain in 2001 by
Orion Media
An imprint of Orion Books Ltd
Orion House, 5 Upper St Martin's Lane,
London WC2H 9EA

A CIP catalogue record for this book
is available from the British Library

ISBN 0 75284 597 7

Typeset by Selwood Systems, Midsomer Norton

Printed in Great Britain by
Butler & Tanner Ltd, Frome and London

To my parents
who gave Perth early pointers
Kay and Otto
who brought her back
and Barbara Stapeley
who saved her

To plains with well-breath'd beagles we repair,
And trace the mazes of the circling hare.

Alexander Pope, 'Windsor Forest'

Chapter 1

When one clear and golden September morning in 1965 we guided our beige Volkswagen bug through the gorgeous countryside of upstate New York to a local kennel to purchase our beagle, we had no way of imagining what was to come. We expected the average expenses and inconveniences but never dreamed of the profound and lasting effects our new companion would have on our lives. With our beagle, my wife Cindy and I would come to endure far greater trials, anxieties, and suffering than most dogs ever inflict on their families. Much of it was our own doing, but this dog would never be a mere pet. She would be more like a force, a way of life, a way of looking at things, a friend, an inspiration, an adventure. She brought us the most intense pleasure, along with the most intense agony.

We were in our mid-twenties, just married. We did not yet want to have children, just a dog. It was a good time for us to buy one. I was in the final year of my Ph.D. in English literature, spending my days at home writing my thesis while Cindy trudged off every day to teach in the local elementary school. Writing is a lonely activity so I thought I would be happy to have a dog's companionship during the day. We lived in a perfect place for a dog, a pretty apartment that had been made out of the loft of a large, wood-framed garage poised picturesquely on the banks of Cazenovia lake, just a mile outside of Cazenovia village, a nineteenth-century Scottish settlement nestled in the soft hills. There were woods and fields everywhere, a lake to swim and canoe in, and an infinitude of rabbits to chase. A dog's paradise.

We wanted a beagle for practical reasons. Beagles are intelligent, spunky, middle-sized with short hair that does not shed over the furniture and carpets, and specifically a member of the hound family that would be a compromise between a lap-oriented dachshund or spaniel and a shuffling, salivating basset hound. A kennel in the woods over in a village by Green Lakes State Park had two or three litters of beagles on offer. We sped over there.

This kennel had a good reputation for breeding beagles, which were especially popular in that northern territory for hunting and tracking. It did not take us long to get there from our lakeside haven. As we walked up to the wire fence that caged fifteen or so pure-bred beagle puppies, about half of them began to bark and howl frantically at us, which beagles do very convincingly. The others were tired and uninterested, passive, their eyes too glazed over with boredom to rouse themselves. As we thrived on peace and quiet, the noisy ones were not for us. But since we also had a taste for adventure, neither would the dull ones do.

'There's no way we're going to choose one of those sluggards,' I said. 'We've got to have an energetic dog.'

'Yes, but not too energetic.'

In the next instant we caught the eye of a puppy who perked up her ears and quietly fixed us in a comprehending gaze. Cindy nudged me, 'Look at that beautiful black one with a brown head, over there on the grass, looking at us. I wish she would come closer.'

The puppy kept looking at us intensely, not yet stirring.

2

I was taken with her beauty, especially the softly rounded brownness of her head and her perfectly white chest and paws. Suddenly, as if sensing in us some sort of kinship, she bounded up and streaked straight towards us through the riot of confusion the other puppies were making. With her paws up on the fence directly in front of us, she looked at us desperately and pleadingly. We touched her head and paws through the fence and knew instantly.

'This is the one, without doubt,' I whispered urgently. 'She wants us, the others don't.'

'And we want her! Let's take her home. Look at her eyes.'

Fifty dollars and ten minutes later her papers were handed over and Cindy had her in her arms, where now she was quiet and contented.

'Oh, one thing before you go,' the burly man who ran the kennel said as we were walking out the door. 'You'd better let me tattoo her ear with your initials. Lots of thefts of dogs in these parts, especially of beagles. Mad scientists like to do vicious experiments on them. They won't touch a dog with a tattoo, though.'

'Will it hurt her?'

'Not a bit.' With that, he slipped my initials, PEM, into his tattooing pliers, delicately placed the puppy's floppy left ear into them, and squeezed. The letters appeared in purple, like veins, inside the ear and out of sight. No sound from the puppy. It took only seconds but years later those would become among the most important seconds in our lives.

There were problems straight away. Our little friend got sick in the car on the way home and chewed up a section of the carpet in the apartment on the first night, but what kept us up most of the night was deciding what to call her.

Her name had to be romantic and imaginative, not trite,

3

commonplace, or the kind of cute and humdrum name that generally makes you feel as if you are breathing stale air in a stuffy room, or the overly clever, affected choice like 'Mozart', or 'Himalaya', or 'Shakespeare'. Also it had to suggest her energy and beauty. And she certainly was beautiful. Slightly smaller and less chunky than the British hunting variety, she was an American 'blanket' beagle, so called because of her solid black back. As the black spread down over her shoulders and haunches, it turned to a golden brown which two-thirds down her legs became the purest white. Her chest was of the same soft white, her short hair combing itself naturally and delicately in various directions, joining in several places like the crest of a breaking ocean wave. It was a pleasure to trace her hair with a finger. Her tail was also black, but tipped off with white at the end. Her silky brown ears, which hung gracefully down to her shoulders as they do incomparably on beagles, framed a smooth, soft brown head except for a thin, white line along the middle of the crown and a delicate line of black around her eyes that really did seem as if someone had applied eye-liner to them.

As Sir Toby Belch said of his beloved Maria in Shakespeare's *Twelfth Night*, this little puppy was 'a beagle, true-bred'. And I hoped that she would have many of Maria's qualities – sauciness and mischievousness, imagination, humour, energy and a refusal to suffer fools gladly. Only time would tell, but the signs were good.

'Although that head is unmistakably feminine, I don't think we should give her a feminine name,' Cindy said at about three in the morning, sipping her tea with the three-month old puppy stretched out on her lap.

'I was thinking the same thing,' I replied, becoming poetic. 'It would be too narrow for her. She needs to travel this earth with a larger identity. She needs a name that does not tie her down to her sex, a distinctive name.'

Then a name suddenly popped into my mind. 'Perth! We'll call her Perth, after Sir Walter Scott's novel, *The Fair Maid of Perth*.' We were just back from an entire summer in Scotland, our minds brimming with its romantic landscape's magic of hills, mountains, lochs, mountain breezes and wild echoes. We had also visited the lovely town of Perth in the Lowlands, on the Great North Road between Edinburgh and Inverness, near the mouth of Scotland's longest river, the Tay. Mild and civilised in its outlook, it has been called the most congenial place to live in Britain. In Scotland, in fact, we found much of the spirit of romance and adventure with which we hoped to keynote our marriage.

My father always thought the name was absurd. How can you call after her with a name like that, he would ask. It does not exactly trip off the tongue. But with her name, Perth received our dream of the future. We fell asleep, with her perfectly at peace somewhere between us on the bed.

In the morning we threw on our bathing suits and walked down the twisting, wooded path to the magical lake. There Perth gave us her first surprise. It was a warm late September Saturday, the water was crystal clear and still warm, the hills circling the lake were bathed in morning sunshine, and the trees were showing early signs of autumnal colour. Perth stood with us on the water's edge, sniffing the air, eyes wide open, all her senses alive to the sensations of her new life. Her little body was sharply defined in the bright air, her head moving briskly this way and that as she caught a succession of delicious scents.

'Let's promise never to live in any place where we have to

tie her up,' I said, my eyes fixed on her. 'She'll always be free to run, and beagles *will* run. I've heard that when they begin to chase rabbits and other game they can run up to four hundred miles in a weekend. They don't look especially powerful, but their supple muscles conceal great strength. Not to mention their great lung power. Apparently they never wear out. Which poet was it who wrote of the "well-breath'd beagles" that "trace the mazes of the circling hare"?'

This theme of freedom was important in our lives. Even before Cindy and I married we knew the kind of life we did not want to live together. Neither of us wanted office jobs. Nor would money be an overriding factor in any decisions we made. As long as we had enough to be comfortable, we preferred a lifestyle that would give us time and space. Would it not be a life misspent to slog it out mechanically and repetitiously, day after day, year after year, in confined spaces pursuing the illusory, conventional pleasures of monetary success? Money can buy lots of things, but could it produce time, the time to go places, see things? If we had lots of money, we could buy lots of fine furniture, but the problem with even the most splendid sofa is that it is not very mobile. To enjoy it you rather have to stay at home. What could be worse than feeling trapped by material possessions? How sterile an existence that would be.

Call such attitudes the idealism of youth, perhaps, but we were highly ambitious – for time, adventure, freedom, and variety. We also told ourselves that if we ever had children, we would try to impart such values to them, too. But now in Cazenovia we had Perth, not children.

'It would be criminal ever to tie her up,' Cindy said, gazing fondly at Perth's brisk, keen movements. 'We chose her because she chose us. Do you think she wanted us because we didn't look like the sort of people who would ever tie her up?'

'Could be. It's good to think so. Imagine her as inheriting the earth, as the Bible says, or at least the natural world. Isn't that the kind of dog we want? One who will be as free as we want to be? How can a dog inherit the earth if she is tied up all the time?'

'Many people will feel it's irresponsible of us never to tie her up, you know,' Cindy replied. 'Why shouldn't we have to keep her on a lead most of the time, they might wonder, if they have to. They'll think we should play by the rules. Also, they'll think we don't care about her safety, that she'll get run over or lost.'

'Something about Perth tells me that if we ever take to tying her up, shutting her up in a room, or restricting her in any way, we'll be in for a lot of trouble. Anyway, I don't think we'd be placing her in any danger if we leave her free.'

'Why not?'

'If you train a dog for the life you intend it to have, just like a child, it will be equipped to deal with that sort of life. I don't think that a dog on a lead thinks for itself as much as one on its own. It's like closing up a part of its mind. By running free Perth will be more alert, more in tune with her instincts. She'll be wary of strangers who might want to harm her and be capable of navigating herself. She is less likely to get lost or run over.'

'I hope so,' Cindy said wistfully.

'And she'll also be lovable. We won't pull her towards us; she'll come to us when she wants to. We won't suffocate her with love.'

'It'll be hugely more fun having a free and adventurous dog, that's for certain.'

'She'll be the way we want ourselves to be.'

'Well, while she's discovering her brave new world,' Cindy shouted, 'let's go for a swim. There won't be too many more warm days like this.'

'Better yet, let's take the canoe out and swim in the middle of the lake.'

We often did this. It gave us a fine view of the shoreline and the air was even fresher out there. Perth had gone off into the woods, sniffing among the previous autumn's leaves, and without any fuss we let her get on with whatever she was doing while we paddled off across the early morning, glittering water, our paddles dipping softly in and out of the water with a rhythmical quietness in tune with the peacefulness of the scene. The lake was six miles long but only one mile wide, and we made for about half way across. There were no other sounds except the songs of birds.

'I wish we never had to move and could stay here for ever,' Cindy whispered after a few minutes, clouded for a moment by the sudden thought that by next summer I would have finished my thesis and would need to find a university teaching job somewhere far away from this lakeside paradise among the tinted hills.

'We're about half way out now,' I piped up. I tucked the paddles into the canoe and gazed back at the shore. 'No sign of Perth; maybe she's down some rabbit hole by now.' I had to squint because of the sun's brilliance, reflected on the water in a riot of dancing bright lights.

'You go first,' I said. Cindy eased her smooth, sun-tanned body into the cooling water. I followed. We swam around the boat, dived under it, floated lazily on our backs. After half an hour I was climbing back into the boat when I heard slurping and breathing behind me. I looked back and there was Perth.

'I don't believe it,' I shouted. Cindy, who was by then dozing in the canoe, sprang up and almost managed to tip it over.

'What's the matter?' she shouted.

'Incredible. We're not alone. What an animal! It's Perth, she swam all the way out here. How wonderful!'

Cindy reached down and took hold of her firmly under her front legs, lifting her into the canoe. Perth shook herself, barked at me as I held on to the side of the canoe, and then walked smartly to the bow where she took up a position on the front seat looking out across the lake. No fuss from her, no puppyish whimpering and endless tail-wagging. It was as if she had asserted herself as a member of a new triumvirate. I climbed back into the canoe and with her still at the prow we paddled slowly back to shore. 'I didn't think a little dog like this could swim so far,' was all Cindy permitted herself to say. I just paddled, staring at the back of Perth's brown head, held high.

The next few days were spent getting to know each other and walking through the woods and meadows along the lake – which Perth relished with a frantic energy. She tracked scents everywhere, yapping delightedly in the distance, out of sight. But she always knew exactly where we were. She did not act like a slight puppy who had passed from womb to cage, and only the day before been released into a new existence.

Except, that is, when she played with the dog next door, a huge St Bernard called Frederick.

Frederick was everything Perth was not: big, slow, predictable, generally slobbery, and with vast amounts of hair.

He was also immensely affectionate. They met often. You could always tell when they had been together because Perth would arrive home with her head saturated from Frederick's saliva. Frederick looked like he could have swallowed Perth in one gulp, but the most dangerous he ever got was to open his jaws wide and close them playfully on her head. As they rolled on the ground, his saliva poured on to her like a warm waterfall. He could do this without any of his teeth leaving the slightest mark on her. She took her revenge by moving off thirty feet or so and then running headlong at him, crashing into his furry side or chest, bouncing off and then repeating the assault. Frederick scarcely felt it and merely salivated more. They were exquisitely fond of each other, but Frederick, with his massive body, could be no part of Perth's life of quickness and exploration. He could only guess at it. He was always tied up. They could never roam together in this dog's paradise. He only slobbered a little more than usual when he saw Perth.

During the autumn months, to relieve my long days at home alone, I began to teach Perth an assortment of clever tricks which she learned with ease.

'Are you spending your time teaching her silly nonsense?' Cindy asked one day when she got home from teaching. She had just seen Perth stand on her hind legs with a slice of sausage on her nose for five seconds without eating it. 'I'm spending my days teaching children how to read and you're training her to be a circus performer!'

'Ah, yes, but unlike many of your pupils, Perth is an incredibly keen learner. There's so much intelligence in her that I feel I've got to tap.'

'How about tapping some of your own pent-up intelligence instead, and getting on with your writing? If you don't finish your thesis by August, you'll miss out on that university job you've been offered. Then we'll be poor and have to sell Perth.'

As she said this, Perth, who was growing impatient with this conversation, tried a few of her tricks to get attention. She performed three consecutive roll-overs, a sit-up, a stand-up, and a lie-down in quick succession.

'Look at that,' I beamed.

'She looks programmed to me. Why did she do all those tricks at once?'

'For emphasis, mostly, as well as because she's hungry and wants another piece of sausage. If one trick doesn't get her what she wants, she tends to try a whole bunch at once.'

'How many tricks have you taught her?'

'Eighteen.'

As if to answer the question, Perth suddenly came out with a series of rhythmic barks.

'For heaven's sake, is that a trick, too? She's not even barking naturally now.'

'Don't worry, she's still in the training stage. She'll soon get them sorted out and then do them only on command. It's good for her, it sharpens her mind.'

'I'm worried about what else it's doing to her mind, not to mention to your own.'

I also spent these months training Perth for more serious things, especially to beware of the perils of roads and traffic. The most common way for a dog to be killed is by a car. The obvious road to start with was the one about one hundred feet from our home, a lonely road but not without its share of mad drivers. I was playful with the tricks, but with this part of Perth's education I was ruthless. My goal was to make her distrust all roads on planet Earth. After training her not to set one paw on the road's surface unless she was with me, I tested her. Standing on one side of it while she waited on the other, I dangled a piece of meat or some other enticing morsel and beckoned to her softly with endearing phrases like, 'What a nice doggie; come with me Perth and let's have a good run. Come on, come here.' Or I would speak more angrily and command her across the road, 'Come here now Perth, you bad dog. Come *here*!' At first, she could not resist crossing the road, but after a week or so she held her ground, resisting everything I could do to lure her across. I then took her into Cazenovia village and, to both the displeasure and amusement of passers-by on the High Street, tested her there, too. This demanded more of her concentration because of the noise and commotion all around, but she soon caught on. Undistracted by people who stopped to watch her she would not budge from the street kerb. This was risky but I was careful and she learned. I succeeded therefore in making her perfectly streetwise. It was a lesson that in the future would save her life many times over.

Chapter 2

That first winter was the worst this part of the country had known for decades. Before Christmas the temperature fell well below zero and stayed there for weeks at a time. The lake froze solid and became a magnificently hard, glassy surface, several square miles of open, perfect ice: a skater's wonderland. You could skate for miles, whizzing along and taking in the views of the rolling hills as you went. Fishermen came on to the lake too, with their ice saws and fishing tackle. They cut holes in the ice, dropped their lines in and waited, every now and again stirring the water in the holes to keep it from freezing over.

We were among the first on the ice. With Perth running and sliding with us, we skated back and forth across the lake and several miles down its length, occasionally stopping along the shoreline to sit on a log to rest or to drink hot tea from our thermos. Perth had grown almost to her full size and, as a result of constantly running freely during the autumn, had developed very strong muscles. It was ecstasy for her on the ice. Her favourite orbit was to run on far ahead, then pause, pivot around, and burst into an explosion of speed right at us, and finally, instead of crashing into us as she did with Frederick, veer to the side in a huge loop that carried her far off again. She did this endlessly, untiringly, a black and brown body with a white chest streaking into widening circles. She

13

seemed in a trance, driven furiously by something that would give her no rest.

As for snow that winter, old folks who had lived in Cazenovia all their lives could not recall ever having had so much. Two feet fell a few days after Christmas – too late for a white Christmas – and it just kept on falling. A storm in late January, which they still call the Great Blizzard, dropped three more feet in a couple of days, so that by February there was more than five feet on the ground, none of it showing any sign of melting. The snow made life miserable for many people, but its shining magic on the hills, trees, farmhouse barns and lake was breathtaking. The entire landscape was frozen into a muffled stillness. All wildlife seemed buried alive. If you could find a ploughed road to walk on, it felt as if you were alone on earth, a solitary being boxed in by walls and layers of white below, beside and above you. It was exquisite.

There was no more skating on the lake that winter after the snow fell, but Perth still coursed over its crusty blanket as best she could, for hours on end. There was a drama to her life in these months, scripted by nature, that she began to take for granted as part of normal existence. Would life always be like this?

As the world began to thaw out in March and April, it was plain that I would finish my degree by midsummer and then we would have to move to the Midwest to take up my new job. Neither of us looked forward to it because it meant the end of our vigil of innocence and freshness that we identified with the embracing beauty of landscape and water, our new and perfect marriage, and the startling presence of Perth as a force and an energy. We felt embraced by youth and hope. Having to trade upstate New York for a relatively flat and prosaic part of Midwestern Ohio seemed unfair. I even thought of giving up the job. As for Perth, she must have thought everywhere was like Cazenovia. We could not picture her anywhere else.

The final summer months by the lake felt like an Indian summer of all that was good, blooming, and delicious. Every day Perth roamed and explored trails for miles through the woodland, pastures, hills and lonely farms, and along rivers and waterfalls and into gardens and golf courses. She had total freedom from dawn to dusk. Often she returned home in the evening with scarcely an ounce of strength left in her limbs. Then she slumbered motionless for hours, only twitching slightly, her eyes rolling as she dreamed of her adventures, sinking deeply into the soft cushions of the armchairs. The remarkable thing was that she always smelled clean. You never had smelly hands after touching her, the way you do with many dogs, even those who are carted off regularly to stylish grooming shops by their owners. Nor did she ever have bad breath, a terrible thing for a dog (and its owners) since it is usually worse than the foulest of human breaths.

She had one enticing aroma, however, that was strangely seductive. It was what we called her groggy-doggie smell. This was an odour unique to her that Cindy, especially, loved. After Perth had been sleeping for a while, or been curled up somewhere, her body took on a warm, cosy, intimate, furry smell – not a dirty or cloying smell such as that of dogs who are not allowed to run outside enough with plenty of fresh air passing through their hair. The groggy-doggie smell, on the contrary, made Perth mysteriously attractive. We seemed to be the only ones who were aware of it, but I often thought that if somehow it could be bottled it could become quite the fashion among the sporting set.

Another endearing quality she had already shown was that she scarcely ever licked us. She clearly had fallen in love with us, but she never slopped her tongue on our hands and faces. Here again she differed from dogs that seem to use their lolling tongues as the only way of communicating, and do it with anyone in range. Once in a long while she would give us a brief lick or two, but she never did it to anyone else. It was not unloving; it was discriminating, a clue to her intelligent devotion and essential lack of sentimentality.

One evening in early July, standing on the pier, watching the shimmering trail of moonlight across the lake, as we savoured the present and wondered about the future, Cindy said, 'Have you noticed that we never worry about Perth? You know, that one day she may be run over, or that some angry farmer will throw a pitchfork at her, or she'll break a leg or lose her way.'

'Perth, lose her way!' I was amused by the thought. 'She was born with a magnetic needle in her head that always guides her safely home. If I am ever lost in a wilderness, I would certainly want to have her with me. It must be more than her sense of smell because she always seems to know where to go without ever having been there before.'

We fell silent. I kept thinking of her unfailing sense of direction. Years later in unhappier times Perth would have to draw on all her instincts and stamina to find her way out of a wilderness and survive, but now all was well and we were at peace with our young world.

Chapter 3

Miserably quickly, the glorious summer ended. I completed my degree and in early September we packed our belongings, mostly books, into a rental truck. Saying goodbye to our friends was less painful than leaving the lake, where we had centred our lives for several years and where in the last year Perth had become a fearless, roaming, even defiant genius of the place. There would be no lake where we were going in the unbeckoning heartland of America.

As we drove out of our driveway through the pine trees, the ground beneath covered with golden pine needles lit up by shafts of sunlight, starting our thousand-mile journey to Ohio, Frederick (who had somehow got loose from his rope) sat motionless watching us go, streams of saliva running out of his mouth and an unmistakable look of aloneness on his face. Perth stared through the back window at him, making no sound, just staring, as if she knew she would never see him again.

It is not necessary to this story to say anything more about our move to Ohio than that we found a pleasant house to rent on the edge of uncompromisingly flat farm fields. Cindy found a teaching job, although she had to drive twenty miles through endless acres of corn and wheat to get there. There were pigs everywhere, it seemed. I settled into my teaching of English literature at the university.

It was a plain and simple life, without any drama of landscape, or drama of any kind except what Perth provided. What we left behind in Cazenovia quickly became, as a poet once said, like the distant 'glory and the freshness of a dream' that now we could see no more. We had been turned out of paradise. Instead of a lake there were smelly pig farms, instead of hills and thick pine woods, straight and dusty roads in between inert and motionless fields. Closer to town there were sterile subdivisions with houses lined up neatly beside each other along treeless drives.

Perth felt the dullness of it all, at a loss as to what to do with herself. At first she began to lose her spirit, as often happens to humans when they are bored. Her behaviour changed. She had complete freedom to go wherever she wanted, but in place of heroic deeds on lakes and treks in wildernesses, she raided dustbins. She drifted over to the pig farms and rolled around in the mud and slop. She also became irritated and started growling at people. She terrified the postman and milkman, howling madly and running straight for them with the hair up on her neck, as if she were going in for the kill. It was all a pretence, of course, for she had never bitten anyone. But they did not know that. What worried us was that her joy and boldness of spirit in the East was turning into a dangerous sort of impatience and intolerance in the Midwest. With us she was fine, but otherwise she seemed angry and disoriented. She mirrored our own feelings a little, though we masked them better than she did.

She shocked us one day by serving notice that she refused to be left alone at home. It was not always possible to let her stay outside. There was a children's birthday party next door and with many toddlers running around outside we thought it best to keep her inside when we went off for a couple of hours. We learned our lesson the hard way. When we got back home, the sitting room was a disaster area. The sofa was completely torn to shreds. In a delirious fury Perth had ripped out all the stuffing, which was spread out all over the floor. There was hardly anything left of the sofa. The carpet was not in much better shape, shredded and ripped along the edges.

So a few weeks later when we went out for an entire day, against our better judgment but compelled to do it because we had heard there was a dog-catcher working the neighbourhood, we decided to keep her in the garage. The garage opened to the driveway with two large, swinging, wooden doors. Returning home at the end of the day, we were surprised to see Perth trotting jauntily up the road about a mile from home, as if she had not a care in the world.

'What is she doing out?' I shouted. 'Someone must have let her out of the garage. Maybe her barking was too much for the neighbours.' We opened the car door and she hopped in, her tail wagging.

Even before we turned into the driveway, we saw the damage. There was a gaping hole in the garage doors. She had eaten and clawed her way through one of them.

'That dog is becoming lethal,' I complained as I approached the door. 'She must have jaws of steel.' Fragments and splinters of wood were all over the place. She had gone about it quietly. The neighbours had heard nothing. But the ferocity of her determination to escape was daunting, as if she had been possessed by the devil.

'She went berserk,' Cindy said, now holding Perth and stroking her gently. 'What's the matter, Perth, what's wrong? You know we'll come back to you. You don't need to do this.'

'She didn't just chew the wood from the door,' I moaned, inspecting the damage. 'It looks like she bit off large chunks and then gnashed away at them all over the garage. And look at these deep gouges she made with her nails. This door won't keep anyone out now. This is getting expensive.'

The next week we left her outside when we went off to work, and this seemed to work. We had no idea what she got up to all day, but at least no debris of splintered wood nor fragments of stuffing or other displaced parts of our house were waiting for us when we got home. Perth won that test of wills. From then on she was much happier. The devil had been somewhat exorcised.

That weekend, though, a new and unexpected side of her character showed itself. On Saturday morning, a crisp and sunny October day, we were outside talking to our neighbours Jim and Mary Jo Clark. Jim had also just joined the English faculty at the university. He taught Shakespeare. He was a bearded, heavy-set young man from Arizona who incongruously combined antiquarian book collecting with motorcycle touring. Parked outside his house next door was his enormous, gleaming, dangerous-looking 850 cc. Moto Guzzi cycle monster. He was amused by our emotional troubles with Perth.

'Don't be too worried about Perth,' he said. 'She'll get over this rebellious mood in three or four years. The question is whether you'll have any money left by then.' A very helpful remark.

Perth was listening to this calmly, a pretty picture of docility.

'Perth's problem is not her age, it's her steely determination and stubbornness,' I replied. 'She's always been that way and doesn't have enough to do around here. There aren't even any dogs in the neighbourhood for her to pal around with. She's bored.'

'She's really a pretty dog,' said Mary Jo, trying to make up for her husband's joke.

I thought I could put him to use. 'Look, Jim, we've got to go into town for a couple of hours and it's really inconvenient to take her with us. But if we don't, she might follow. I don't suppose you could hold her until we're well away, could you, just for a couple of minutes? Then you can let her go and she'll stick around.'

'Sure, anything to help a desperate colleague.'

I saw him in the rear view mirror crouched down and holding on to Perth as we drove off. She was looking intently after us.

Two hours later we returned. Perth was waiting on the front porch, delighted to see us. I immediately went next door to thank Jim, who answered the door holding a large bloodstained handkerchief in his hand. His nose had spots of blood on it.

'What happened to your nose?' I asked, trembling a little.

'Your dog bit me. As soon as you were out of sight, she twisted to get free and when I gripped her more firmly she turned round and took a chunk out of my nose, fast as lightning.'

'Oh, no. Is it bad? Does it hurt? I'm truly sorry, Jim. This is awful.'

'For a moment I didn't know what had happened. It was a neat bit of work, very clinical. It didn't hurt. I saw the blood and let her go. I exaggerated, it's not that serious, but noses bleed a lot. She really wanted to go after you, I'll tell you that.'

'She's never bitten anyone before,' I said weakly. I could

see there were two neat little tooth marks on either side of the bridge of his nose. 'Can I do anything for you, Jim?' I added anxiously.

'Never mind, it's just two little punctures. She didn't want to eat me up, just wanted to send me a message. Anyway, she doesn't have rabies, does she?'

Those were days before suing even your best friends became a national pastime in America. Jim was polite and unconcerned. I, on the other hand, felt sick.

He consoled me. 'Come in and have a Coke and let's forget about it. Some dog that. Really attached to you. She really looks sweet until you try to make her do something she doesn't want to do. If I were you, I'd warn people not to put their noses close to her head.'

Cindy worried. That night she said, 'This is a problem. We can't have her biting our friends. How can we remember to tell all our guests, the moment they step through our front door, not to put their heads close to her?'

'It's just that she doesn't like it here. She's bound to get used to it. We've known from the beginning she's not an average kind of dog. We'll have to be careful, that's all.'

Very troubled, we eventually went off to sleep, with Perth as usual sleeping on the end of our bed. But she continued to snap at people in Ohio, though only twice more making contact with noses. 'No, don't put your head down to her,' I shouted frantically as a colleague called Jerry one day recklessly rushed over to her in an armchair and lowered his head towards her. It was too late. Frighteningly fast, Perth grazed his prominent nose with her teeth, immediately drawing some blood. I heard it, not saw it. He was good-natured about it, but the poor man left in some agitation.

We did not have much time to worry more about Perth

because the following Monday morning a tragedy struck. Cindy left for work preoccupied with the especially heavy day she had ahead of her, so she was not concentrating entirely on her driving. About five miles from home, on one of the winding farmland back roads she used as a shortcut, she allowed the car to drift into the lane of oncoming traffic as she swept around a bend. At that time of the morning on those narrow, quiet roads, there was hardly any traffic, but at exactly that moment a car rushed towards her around the bend. They collided. Fortunately it was not a head-on collision, but it was very close to it.

I was in the kitchen at home talking to Perth when a policeman rang the doorbell. Perth howled wildly as she did whenever anyone rang the bell.

'Are you Peter Martin, husband of Cindy Martin?' he asked.

'Yes.'

'You'll have to come with me to the hospital,' he said coldly, 'your wife has had a car accident.'

Perth was standing next to me when the policeman said this, and immediately she stopped wagging her tail. A horrible chill ran through me and for a few moments I said nothing. It was a feeling of desperation such as I would never care to have again. I feared the worst, imagining that our world had suddenly collapsed, and along with it all our plans and dreams.

'Someone hit her?' was all I could manage.

'I'll tell you the details on our way. It wasn't as bad as it might have been.'

'Stay here, Perth.' Perth understood the tone of that command and sat quietly as I left. She waited all day.

The policeman asked several questions on the way, but I

was afraid to ask him any. Instead, I prayed. I am religious and especially at times like this I always feel that God is close to us. We walked into the hospital. The smells of the place worried me. I had been in a hospital only once before. It seemed an alien place, cold and metallic. I was directed down a corridor and was half way down it when a door opened and Cindy was wheeled out on her way to the operating room. She was fully conscious and, typically, was grinning broadly, which looked incongruous with the cuts on her lovely features. I could not hide the pained look on my face.

'Don't worry, dear,' she said, 'it's just a broken leg. They're going to operate on the leg now. It doesn't hurt. And all my face needs is a minor stitch or two.'

Holding her hand, all I could say was, 'See you soon. I love you.'

'I love you, too.' They had started down the corridor with her when she added, 'Where's Perth?'

'She's fine, at home. She was very quiet when I left. She seemed to know something was amiss.'

Cindy smiled, and they continued on with her toward the operating theatre.

An hour later a nurse told me they had decided to delay the operation for a few weeks. But they had fixed up Cindy's cuts. 'Go home now,' she said to me, 'she's asleep. Come back around dinner time.'

Frank Jordan, our best new friend in the English department, a gracious bachelor from North Carolina, had by then joined me in the hospital.

'Come and have lunch with me, Peter, and we'll talk,' he said. 'You need to be with someone.'

'Thanks, Frank, but I can't. I really should be with Perth.' I felt it would do me the most good to be with her.

'Well then, have dinner with me this evening.' I agreed and drove home.

Perth was quietly waiting for me. I hugged her on the grass, for a long time. She knew something was dreadfully wrong. She could tell. This was not the first time I had sought consolation and comfort from her in this way. In Cazenovia, whenever my writing was giving me trouble or when I was worried about our future, or even if there were smaller problems, I let her know what was troubling me. People who have never had relationships like this with dogs may think this kind of behaviour in a grown man is sentimental and childish nonsense. I myself may have thought so before I found Perth because all the dogs in my family while I was growing up were mere pets to me, to cuddle, take for walks, feed and pat on the head. Perth, on the other hand, had become a saving grace, friend and comforter – and never more than at this moment. She was hugely reassuring. She took me out of myself. Instinctively, on some mysterious level of understanding and communication, she knew what she was doing.

After a long walk with her in the afternoon by the pigs and corn, dreaming of better days in Cazenovia, I took her with me to Frank's house. I could not bear to leave her behind. It was early and Frank was not yet home, so I hurriedly left her alone in his house before walking over to the hospital. I found Cindy's room and peeked in. Her leg was suspended high in some complicated apparatus. I decided to be light-hearted at all costs.

She was jubilant when she saw me. 'Oh, come in, I've been longing to see you. Where've you been?'

'Well, you're still in one piece, I see, even if you're in an odd shape. They told me not to come before now. Are you in any pain?'

'None at all. I'll have to stay in traction for three weeks, though, before they can operate on my leg. I don't know if I can take that. I'll go crazy!'

I was shocked, but sitting down and taking her hand, I said gently, 'They have ways of making you comfortable, don't worry. And think of all the reading you'll get done – the time will pass quickly, you wait and see.'

Her eyes glistened with tears. We talked for some minutes more and then she asked, 'How's Perth?'

'As a matter of fact, she's only a couple of blocks from here. Frank invited me to dinner and I brought her along. I couldn't leave her, not tonight. She misses you. We took a long walk together this afternoon.'

'I wish I could see her.'

I suddenly had an uneasy feeling as I thought of Perth in Frank's house, without Frank there. Perhaps I should have left her outside. But surely she would never damage the inside of someone else's house. If she did escape from the house somehow, where would she go?

'Peter, what's the matter?'

'I think I'd better do a quick check on Perth. I keep hearing in my mind the tearing of wood and the muffled sound of billowing chair stuffing.' I had another ghastly thought as I remembered Frank's antique Persian carpets. 'I'll be right back.'

'But I've got so much I want to tell you. Can't Perth wait?'

'I don't think so. Really, I'll be back in a flash.'

I kissed her and walked towards the door, but before I reached it Perth trotted in, her little nails clicking delicately on the tiled floor, her tail wagging wildly, her head jauntily held up, as if she were thinking, 'I can get in wherever I want.' We both saw her at the same moment. I was speechless with amazement.

'Perth!' Cindy shouted. 'My little doggie. Come here, come here, you precious, naughty hound.'

Perth made for her on the bed like a shot. She had the sense not to bark or howl. Landing on the bed, this time with a sense of occasion, she gave Cindy three or four licks.

I was torn between delight and guilt. To have Perth on Cindy's bed was therapy that the doctor could never prescribe. It was richer medicine than he had in his bag of tricks. But dogs were not supposed to be in hospitals. The nurses would attack me if they found her here. Where *were* the nurses?

'How did she get in here? We're on the third floor, for heaven's sake! How did she find us?'

She had jumped out of one of Frank's open windows, I later found out, and apparently followed my scent to the hospital. The sliding entrance doors were open on nice days, so she slipped in unseen and followed the scent by the reception desk, up two flights of stairs, by the nurses' desk in Cindy's ward, down the corridor, and into the room. Since nobody followed her in, it seemed nobody saw her.

I locked the door and relaxed in the general merriment. Cindy's colour returned and her spirits soared. She had a kind of healing at that moment.

Fifteen uninterrupted minutes of undiluted joy passed and then we had to plan Perth's escape. There was no container to put her in, so after Cindy gave her a few last hugs, I wrapped her in a blue hospital blanket and walked out into the corridor as nonchalantly as I could holding the bundle under my arm. I had to walk by the nurses' desk.

'Got to go now,' I said to one of them at the desk, smiling. 'I'll be back at eight.'

'Not so fast, Dr Martin, I need you to sign a form please.'

'Could I do it this evening? I'm rather in a rush now.'

'It'll only take a minute. It has to be done before I go off duty.'

The only thing I could think of was the toilet.

'Well, may I go in there first?' I motioned to the Gents room.

She nodded. I took Perth inside one of the toilet stalls and uncovered her.

'You must stay here, Perth, for two minutes, without speaking,' I said with some feeling. 'If you don't, your goose is cooked, and so is mine. And you won't be able to see your mistress here anymore. Stay here, do you understand?'

Knowingly, she looked at me, perfectly still. I walked out to the desk and signed the papers.

'Thank you very much,' said the nurse, looking straight at me searchingly.

'Oh, wouldn't you know it,' I replied, looking at the Gents, 'I forgot my blanket in there.'

I walked back in. Perth was still waiting quietly in the stall. I wrapped her up again and walked out, not daring to look at the nurse. I didn't release Perth from the blanket until I was around the corner, out of sight of the hospital entrance. She ran the rest of the way straight to Frank's house; I walked slowly after.

A few hours later at home, depression got the better of me. Perth had lifted our spirits in this crisis like nothing or nobody else could have, but I felt the shock and tension of the day. Not yet two months into our new lives and jobs and this had to happen. Cazenovia seemed a lifetime away, an irrecoverable idyll.

Friends and family rallied round us in the following days and weeks. My brother even flew his plane down from Chicago to see us. Cindy had one or two teeth repaired so that she was as presentable as ever, and she entertained a steady stream of visitors from the university. I eased into a new routine of teaching, cooking and visiting the hospital for a few hours in the late afternoon and evening. For the first time since my marriage I was spending nights without my wife and I did not like it.

Our car had been destroyed beyond repair, so I bought a motor scooter to get to the college. I had meant to do that anyway, before the accident. On the first morning I used it, I arrived at eight o'clock, taught two classes, talked to a few students in my office, and was about to leave to go and see Cindy when Frank popped his head into my office.

'How did you manage to juggle Perth here on your scooter?' he asked.

'What do you mean?'

'Perth is outside, by your scooter, waiting for you.'

'She can't be,' I shouted, jumping up from my chair. 'I didn't bring her here. It's two miles here from home and she doesn't know the way.' Or does she? I thought to myself. 'Besides, scooters surely can't leave enough of a scent for a dog to follow. It must be somebody else's dog who just happens to be sitting next to my scooter.'

Frank was amused. 'Come on, I know what she looks like, it's Perth. I can see it now – you'll never be able to hide from her. She'll track you to the ends of the earth.'

We hurried outside and there she was, sitting demurely in the bright October sunshine, very correctly, very patiently, not drawing any attention, looking closely at everyone who passed by. She was beautiful, with snow-white paws and chest, elegant head, and the deepest brown and black playing over the rest of her body. Recognising me immediately, although there was a crowd of people around the door, she trotted over to me. I bent over, grabbed her shoulders and lifted her up on to her back legs, resting my forehead against hers and staring into her eyes. I loved doing that. She looked back into my eyes, deeply.

'How did you find me, you hound? You've never been here before. This won't do, Perth, you really mustn't track me down everywhere.'

She barked twice and walked around the scooter triumphantly. I sat down on the scooter with her on my lap, and holding her with my left arm I started the engine and drove off across campus towards home, a fairly eccentric sight not unnoticed by several of my students. It was not the last time I had to take her home like that.

As it turned out, Perth played a large part in my visits to the hospital. I reasoned that if I could smuggle her out of the hospital, I should be able to smuggle her in. All I needed was her co-operation. I first tried a spacious zip-up bag with large handles, the kind professional tennis players use. She barely fitted into it.

'My dogge,' Cindy exclaimed, when I pulled Perth out of the bag in her room, taking her in her arms. Instead of 'doggie', we had taken sometimes to calling her 'dogge' in the medieval style of English, which I had been teaching my students – pronounced as if the final 'e' were an 'a'. I also called Cindy 'wyfe', again with the 'a' ending; and she called me 'housbonde'. It may sound nutty to others, but to us it was preferable to names such as 'babe', 'jewel', 'sweetheart', and 'precious'.

'Ah, she smells great, she even has the groggy-doggie smell.

I wish I could keep her here to cover up all these hospital smells. The bag's a great idea.'

'It won't work again. It's too small. She began to whine by the desk out there.'

Perth had stretched out on the bed, pressing herself next to her mistress's good leg and looking in a puzzled way at the strange apparatus suspending the broken leg.

'Won't the blanket work?'

'I can't very well keep bringing in a blanket under my arm. Besides, I'm afraid she'll move her head.'

'Or her tail. Well, it's beautiful being all together. I look forward to it so much.' We could hear lawnmowers at work outside, and the sounds of children playing in a nearby garden. Everything out there was going on as normal.

'How are you coping?' I asked her. 'Are you sore?'

'Mainly restless. If it weren't for the reading I do, I'd go crazy. Television is useless during the day, and even for much of the night. The nurses massage me and help in all kinds of ways. They are so sweet – they'd do anything to make my life easier.'

I tried other ways of smuggling Perth. One that did not work was to strap her to my stomach and wear a large jacket to conceal her. The problem with this was that I could not keep her from slipping down. Eventually, I reverted to the blanket. Nobody noticed or questioned anything, so I stayed with it for the last two weeks.

The operation, when it came, was a success, and a few days after that Cindy was released, four weeks after the accident. On the last morning, Frank and a couple of other friends joined us in her room and we celebrated with a few toasts to health and longevity – Frank smuggled the beverage in, although it was nothing too scandalous for a hospital room.

31

As we walked down the corridor by the desk, Cindy on crutches and I with her suitcase in hand, we paused to thank and say goodbye to the four nurses on duty. Then came the surprise. As we were leaving, one nurse, with a broad smile on her face, piped up rather loudly, 'Your dog is so well behaved, by the way. I love beagles. Bring her back one of these days so we can all meet her.'

I stared at her, acutely embarrassed. Cindy lowered her head. All that eventually came out was a feeble, 'Okay, we will, yes'. Perth had been a well-kept secret, but it was not just we who had kept it. This had been an example of healing in the hospital, a more powerful agent of healing in this case than all the cold and expensive machinery and apparatus on offer. It was, in fact, simple, quiet love. The nurses had understood.

Chapter 4

By the following March, Cindy was stable enough on her feet to resume teaching. A teaching job had come up in town, so from then on she was able to get to work in less than ten minutes without any more worries about a long drive. The months passed and the summer holidays came. We decided to get away from home for the summer by travelling across the country to southern California, then up to British Columbia, and back to Ohio in time for the beginning of the term in September, camping all the way.

This journey was not without its emergencies, and Perth was at the centre of all of them. She was 'lost' several times during the ten weeks, or at least so *we* thought at the time. *She* probably did not. On the first day, we had driven on for an hour after stopping at a petrol station in Illinois, only to discover that Perth was not in the back seat as we had thought she was. We turned around and drove back, muttering to ourselves. She was waiting patiently by one of the petrol pumps. She hopped into the car nonchalantly, undisturbed, without much outward show of emotion, as if to say, 'What kept you?'

Another awkward moment was at the Harry S. Truman Museum in Missouri. When we got back to the car after visiting the museum, Perth was gone. No amount of searching turned her up. It was drawing near closing time, after two hours of hunting for her, when Cindy also discovered that her watch had fallen off her wrist somewhere. Irritated, she strode into the museum again to look for it. She turned a couple of corners and entered a cool and empty room with an exhibition featuring the Korean War. The first thing she heard as she came in was a clicking noise on the tiled floor. There was Perth sniffing around contentedly, appearing to be interested in the museum exhibits displaying pictures of President Truman, General Douglas MacArthur and battle scenes of the war. There was no telling how long she had been in there, but Cindy was in a foul mood.

'What kind of animal are you?' she stormed. 'We should have been half way across this state by now, but here you are, you deplorable hound, sniffing around this museum while we exhaust ourselves for two hours trying to find you.'

Perth watched her, looking a little guilty, perhaps.

'I can't believe nobody has seen you in here. You're a bad dog and I'm beginning to think we should have left you at home in a kennel.'

They walked out of the museum together, past the guards who told Cindy in no uncertain terms the not very surprising news that dogs were not allowed in the museum.

'This is a place for people, lady, not dogs,' said one indignantly.

Instinctively, Cindy defended Perth. 'There is no sign saying that,' she shot back combatively.

'There are some things we don't think we need to have signs for, lady. Do you always take your dog into museums?'

'Always.'

With that, Cindy brushed past him and hastily made for the car with Perth trotting along beside her, leaving the guard fuming behind. In the meantime, I had found the watch in the car. We drove off at last.

For the next week we drove through the beautifully rolling wheat fields of Kansas and over the majestic Rocky Mountains in Colorado with their wild flowers and flowing crystal streams and waterfalls. We saw the orange and rusty splendour of the Grand Canyon, made our way through the spectacular landscape of Mesa Verde and eventually reached the Joshua Tree National Park in the Mojave Desert of south-eastern California. We camped there, careful to zip up the net to keep out scorpions and snakes of the venomous kind. The Mojave Desert is relatively small, but it is serious business. A rocky and scrubby wasteland of low mountains and broad valleys, its daytime summer temperatures normally reach 130 degrees Fahrenheit. Its most famous feature is the aptly named Death Valley, which we decided to give a miss.

We continued westward, down to Tijuana, Mexico, then up the California, Oregon and Washington coasts to British Columbia, and back to Ohio over the Rockies and across the North Central Plains. Perth did not create any major crises, although she was the central protagonist in several anxious moments. She had a fight with a Mexican mongrel in Tijuana that reminded me of a scene from a Graham Greene short story. Scruffy men whiling away the hours in cafés around the square simply watched as Perth raised a little dust in chasing off the presumptuous Mexican cur. A day or two later and in another world, outside Los Angles, we were asked to leave the famous English Garden at the Huntington Library and Museum in San Marino, California, after Perth gobbled up prize strawberries in the decorative kitchen garden. In San Francisco, in the famous Haight-Ashbury intersection, Mecca for the world's hippies, Perth sat placidly (perhaps even dumbfounded) watching the constant procession of incredibly strange-looking human beings. Hippies paraded by in all shapes, with hair of every colour known to man, and in weird and wonderful clothing that would make even today's fashion designers run for cover. They stopped to smoke who knows what and we saw a few of them jabbing away at each other in the bright sunshine with frighteningly dirty needles. Perth could not resist sniffing a few of them, much to their irritation, as she had never encountered anything like their aromas in the many miles she had logged during her short life. I tremble to think what might have happened if she had snapped at one or two of them. They might have taken to jabbing her, launching her on quite a different sort of 'trip'.

More worrying, in Vancouver, British Columbia, we had to decide what to do with her while we took the ferry for a few hours to Victoria Island. The ferry operators prohibited dogs on the boats, and it seemed too much of a bother to try to smuggle her onboard. It was cruel of us, but we parked the locked car in the peaceful shade of a spreading oak and left her in it with the window down about eight inches. She would be cool, we told ourselves, and could sleep away the time. There was a bowl of water on the floor.

We then hastened on to the ferry and waited as the ropes were untied from the dock.

'I feel rotten,' I said, looking at Cindy. 'And guilty. We should have brought her with us. What could we have been thinking of? She'll die of dehydration.' I imagined the worst. She would raise such a rebellious hue and cry that the police would be called in to investigate. They would remove her to some city dog compound and as the weekend was coming it would be days before we could retrieve her.

Cindy did not answer, but her expression said she felt the

same thing. The mountains towered high above the city, the water was the cleanest blue and the island looked green and inviting on the horizon. We stood on the deck by the gangplank as the minutes ticked by, gazing hypnotically down the length of the dock. As a couple of dockers began to throw the ropes on to the ferry, suddenly I saw Perth, or was it a phantom, fly on to the far end of the dock and race towards us at a furious pace. The boat had just begun to ease away as she sprinted for all her worth, a blur as she flew across the weathered boards.

'Good God,' I whispered to Cindy, 'it's Perth.'

It was obvious what was in her mind, but there was no way she could make it. She just kept coming. We were about four feet off the dock when she reached the end of it. Without pausing, she launched herself off the edge and into the air, across the water and on to the boat. The passengers who witnessed her leap through space as if there were no tomorrow, burst into applause when she landed and walked over to us, her tail wagging deliriously. Her little heart was beating wildly. Her eyes were flashing. I looked at her in disbelief and admiration. We kept her out of sight and did our successful smuggling routine on the way to the island and back. It was a glorious day among the flowers and graciousness of Victoria, the climax of our journey.

Cindy and I had begun to take this sort of stunt of Perth's for granted by then, almost as if we had become believers in a type of supernatural wisdom and courage in her. She could never be lost. She was indestructible. We made our way back home with the three of us intact.

Chapter 5

Although life back in Ohio continued to bore us, we enjoyed our second year there more, cementing friendships with people like Frank that we would treasure forever after. Still, we knew we had to move on soon. We could not bear the thought of waking up there twenty years later, expecting that the next twenty years might be spent the same way, a universe away from a large body of water and without hills and mountains. So when after Christmas I was offered an excellent job at a university on the south-east coast of Florida, I jumped at it. By midsummer we were there, reluctant to have left our Ohio friends but eager to embrace the more vivid subtropical climate and the majesty of the ocean, even if Florida had no hills.

I stood on the beach alone on our first morning in Florida as the dawn spread out across the sky, lighting up the ocean in a succession of glorious tints, from a cold and pale grey to an orange-blue, to a triumphant golden glow suffusing the sky, ocean and palm-tree-decked landscape with a reassuring warmth and sense of hope. The sound of the surf made me feel as if I were standing at the edge of the world. Nothing on land behind me seemed real. Gazing out at the ocean, which I had always loved, I felt in a way that I had come home – 'Whereon rolled the ocean, thereon was his home,' Byron wrote. I had not lived by the ocean for fifteen years, not since I was ten, living along the sandy, piny coast of Uruguay, a lifetime ago, before my family had ripped me from the landscape of my youth to move to America.

But the beauty and celebration of that dawn seemed to mock the way I really felt. Cindy and I soon discovered that we had not really landed in a paradise of hope and promise. Florida was even flatter than Ohio, and its culture seemed odd to us. It was America and yet seemed wholly unlike the rest of the country, an American retirement subculture with its own pensioners' logic. Things have changed now, but many young people then felt they were interlopers, only tolerated as guests who did not really belong, useful append-ages to the main business of creating arcadias for the millions in their twilight years. Even at the university, I felt like part of a service personnel for the millions of retired folk who washed over Florida in waves every year. Much of Florida's lifestyle, from bingo games and shuffleboard courts to sterile and spick and span condominiums, seemed totally irrelevant to us.

We arrived in Florida with a large self-drive truck crammed with our chattels, not knowing a soul. It was wretchedly hot and even more wretchedly humid. Perth, I am sure, did not have a clue what was going on. It seemed an empty world with no meaning for any of us. We realised with horror that we may have turned our backs on life itself. I could not even imagine the existence of a decent library here with books telling of the riches of world culture, art and civilisation. Everything was different: smells, sounds, lawns, bugs, birds, fish, vegetation, architecture and the tempo and temper of life itself in the languid and oppressive atmosphere. We were lucky enough to find a reasonable holiday apartment for as long as we wanted it, about two hundred metres from the ocean, within earshot of the surf. But except when we escaped to the beach, we were imprisoned in the air-conditioned apartment, driven to it by the intense heat and humidity.

Cindy and I would have been in despair had it not been for each other, Perth and the ocean. That part of the coast, about twenty miles south of Palm Beach, was extremely wealthy, and the small town, almost a village, we had chosen was blessed with a narrow four-mile-long strip of gorgeous sandy beach studded with enormous mansions and gloriously luxuriant gardens. We were at the humbler end of this stretch. The thick, tangled vegetation completely concealed these houses from the beach. All one could see from the sand was a wilderness of cabbage palms, royal palms, Scotch pines, masses of oleander, hibiscus and other shrubs, long grasses and the scrub kind of vegetation that can always be found fringing a beach.

Perth was the first to come to terms with our new home in Delray Beach. While we unpacked, she made straight for the ocean and in minutes had vanished into the thick labyrinthine undergrowth along Ocean Drive. From time to time we heard her barking and howling as she frenetically chased who knows what. A few hours later she returned, exhausted and lacerated with scratches from sharp and pointed cacti but with the gleam of discovery in her excited eyes.

'Seems like Perth likes it here,' I said.

'I can't imagine what there is for her to explore here, except the beach,' Cindy said lazily, pausing in her making of the beds to notice that Perth was, indeed, very happy. 'Let's go for a swim with her after breakfast tomorrow morning. She can frisk along the surf among the sandpipers. I don't want to do anything but relax after that horrendous drive we've just had.'

It was a beautiful morning, cooler and peaceful. A little breeze caressed the morning air, which was perfectly clear without the normal punishing humidity of that time of year. Vivid colours shone everywhere. The ocean was brilliant, the sun sparkling on it in millions of little gemlike reflections. Surf rolled in gently, hissing pleasantly over the hard-packed sand. Our spirits rose. Instead of breakfasting at home, we decided to treat ourselves in a little yellow-canopied outdoor café just to the north of where the dense strip of mansions and greenery began. The café faced the ocean, and from it we could look in between some towering palms to the shimmering water. Not many people were about. Perth sat quietly next to us as we devoured our bacon and eggs and drank the local nectar, the most delicious freshly squeezed orange juice either of us had ever tasted.

Afterwards the three of us drifted down to the water's edge and walked south along the beach, away from the public area in the direction of the 'wilderness' section of beach. We continued on half a mile or so over the fine white sand between the surf and the thick greenness. We had the beach almost entirely to ourselves since people generally did not go that far to swim and lie out on the sand, preferring instead to be nearer each other and the shops of the public beach. It's a curious thing about human nature, how people like to bunch themselves into crowds instead of striking off on their own.

Perth declined to follow us into the water and ran off in the opposite direction, into the dense undergrowth on the prowl for rabbits, armadillos, racoons and who knows what else. We swam, walked on the beach, and sunned ourselves over the next four hours. Occasionally in the distance we heard her high-pitched howl over the surf. When it came time to leave, she was nowhere in sight. Nor could we hear her. For half an hour I walked along the edge of the beach, yelling her name into the thick vegetation, but nothing came of it. I am sure the crème de la crème sitting on opulent terraces sipping their exotic juices amid their bougainvillea heard me, and a few of the more intuitive among them may even have made the connection between Perth's clamour and my cries. Nobody came out either to help or shut me up, so I gave it up. I paced through the sand back to Cindy.

'Why don't we go home and come back for her later when she's exhausted and ready to quit?' I said hoarsely. We were not worried. Nor was I irritated. In fact, I rejoiced in Perth's good fortune to be able to run and explore at will, to gratify her urges, especially in this environment where things were neat and controlled, where there was little space for pioneering. I had already seen and felt enough of Florida to decide that Perth could be my alter ego, my mouthpiece of protest, my rebel on the move. I would encourage her to be wild. If she could no longer range in romantically rural upstate New York, she could at least disturb some of the enervating tameness here. It is an understatement to say she would be worlds apart from the ubiquitous poodles who made regular visits to the 'poodle-puff' grooming centres around every corner.

We drove back to the apartment. That evening, after dinner, before we set out to find her, she appeared. Tired, limping a little, but obviously happy, she slumped down on the patio. Food and drink soon restored her.

For three months we stayed in this apartment until we bought a house on the west side of the so-called Inland Waterway, a canalised river about half a mile from the coast that cut its way hundreds of miles to the north. We could not afford to buy on the east side of this posh waterway. Perth did not like the move because our new house was in a predictable, neatly laid-out residential area about three miles from the ocean, with much complicated traffic and a huge drawbridge over the waterway in between. Our address did not exactly take one's breath away: Northwest 4th Avenue. We had little choice. There was nothing remotely natural about any of the residential areas. And we had to buy because renting was killing our finances. We were expecting to spend at least three years in Florida.

We had been in residence a week when on the way back from the university one day I stopped in at our former apartment to see if there was any post for us there. Perth, not post, was waiting for me. She was sitting by the pool but there were signs on her that she had been doing the rounds of mansion land again. But to run across town and over the drawbridge, for which she would certainly have had to sit and wait, and then find the apartment, was no small feat. It was a confusing and dangerous route. There did not seem to be anything she could have relied on for direction. I still do not know how she did it. But there she was. I took her back to the beach for a swim. Exhausted, this time she simply sat and gazed out to the sea or contented herself in playing with the tiny sandpipers in the surf while I bodysurfed the waves.

As luck would have it, Perth found a kindred spirit in her new neighbourhood on 4th Avenue, a beagle called Sam, about her size with similar markings but much rougher in appearance. She had some of Perth's spirit but little of her beauty. Perth was now four and, if anything, had become more beautiful, her ears even softer and longer, her eyes more intense and knowing, her black back more glistening. I loved to stroke her but not possessively, knowing when to stop before she told me. A favourite habit of mine in a lazy mood, in a chair with her, was to run my fingers along her ribs, counting them one by one. She loved it. She also melted when I rubbed her shoulders, digging gently into the muscle. One thing I never did was fuss with her ears. She disliked it.

Sam was not a Frederick, but like Perth he ran free, if only through the neighbourhood. Where they went I do not know, but for a few months he was a good companion. It all came to a tragic end one day. Sam may never have been taught properly how to cross streets. He was careless. From inside the house I heard the car's screeching brakes when it hit him. Waiting at the side of the road, Perth watched helplessly as Sam walked straight into the car's path. His howling in pain was horrible. When I got there, Perth was hunched over him trying to lick his wounds. I gingerly gathered Sam up off the pavement on to a sheet, careful not to place my hands near his head. I remembered that when I was a boy in Argentina my brother had tried to grab our dog who had just been run over by a lorry, to pull him off the road. Normally very docile, in his agony our Scottie sunk her teeth deep into his hand and refused to let go, leaving a wide gash that needed thirty stitches. There was nothing I could do for Sam except rush him off to the vet. Perth came with me. But Sam was broken in several places and in acute pain. The vet quickly put him to sleep. We drove home slowly and sadly. I asked myself whether I should stop letting Perth run free, but I quickly put the thought out of my mind. She had proven herself hundreds of times over by then. What was the point of worrying? Besides, to be tied up would be for her a hell on earth, a life not worth living.

There was never another dog in Florida who would befriend Perth. How could she carry on with dogs who were never allowed out of their premises? She reverted to solitary exploration. Occasionally we took her to inland Florida where she coursed through swamps, frightened white herons and even sneaked up on otters on a cattle ranch. She succeeded in avoiding poisonous snakes, including rattlesnakes, water moccasins and cottonmouths, not to mention crocodiles sunning themselves on banks. Other than that, we all endured Florida as well as we could, and as the weeks moved on and the summer holidays approached, we realised we needed to travel to England for several months, where I yearned to do some research.

A research trip to England, however, posed obvious problems. In the first few years of teaching, I had not written enough about my field. My heavy teaching schedules had left me little time for writing. And when I had time, I was often too exhausted. Yet, to write about literature was something I very much wanted to do. Not so that I could obtain tenure, keep from 'perishing' in the academic marketplace and get a higher salary, but simply because I wanted to immerse myself in the subject. If I was unable to do that, I knew I would be very unhappy. Teaching, which I loved, was not enough.

For me, England was the place to do the research, the 'El Dorado' of literary scholarship. And yet, how could we set off overseas and leave our dear Perth for three months? It would be expensive and impractical to take her with us, but if we left her behind it would be a betrayal of trust. We would no longer be worthy of her. She could even permanently lose faith in us. The bond between us might be broken. Perhaps I should just give up all thoughts of scholarship and writing. It seemed an insoluble dilemma. Endless nights we could not sleep for worry over it.

Painfully, at last, we decided to leave her with some close

friends who loved her and with whom we knew at least she would be safe and well cared for, if not happy. Our remorse over leaving her behind would last the whole summer.

Chapter 6

The term ended in May and though we parted gloomily from Perth, leaving Florida was like returning to the real world. Florida had by now become our personal 'heart of darkness', a place far away from the real world, where we felt shut off from mainstream culture and events. At Kent State University, students had actually been shot dead on campus demonstrating against the Vietnam War, yet that news in our Florida cocoon scarcely stirred the placid waters of my university. The ominous drumbeat of a cultural revolution seemed to have started up north, with young people questioning authority at every level, yet in Florida it all seemed irrelevant.

The summer passed quickly and profitably. Our reunion with Perth in September was one of those rich moments in earthly existence when everything seems right and complete again. There was general rejoicing. We found her safe but plump. Too much food and no exercise had taken its toll. Her eyes, too, had a glazed look to them from staying inside so much, keeping cool in the air-conditioning. Afraid of something happening to her, our friends had done what they thought best by keeping her strictly controlled. Her main excitement had been watching racoons through a window. With hindsight, I thought it was a miracle she did not tear the place apart. It was our friends' love and kindness, I think, that kept her calm. Soon we were home, though, and Perth was racing along the beach and molesting the mansions once again. For nine more months we repeated the enervating Floridian cycles of our first year there. Then the next summer was suddenly upon us, and again we had to go to England, for the same reason. There was the same wrench, but this time, our more imaginative search for Perth's temporary home would turn into the Big Adventure of all our lives.

We were determined not to leave her in Florida with the heat and bugs. If we could not take her with us to England, at least we could salve our consciences somewhat by finding somewhere up in the north where we knew she would be cool, out of the sticky Floridian humidity, and in rolling countryside that would beckon to her adventurous spirit. Instead of flying directly to London from Miami, therefore, we drove one thousand miles north, hoping to find in Ohio responsive old friends with short memories who could be prevailed on to take her for the summer. Failing that, we could push on eastward to Cazenovia and search there. All being well, we would then fly from Boston where Cindy's parents, the Peters, lived in a high-rise block of apartments in the Back Bay area, next to the Prudential Centre. The journey would also be for us a symbolic migration backwards in our married life, back to our original landscape in Cazenovia, our Garden of Eden, where the world seemed simpler and more innocent.

Ohio was certainly no Eden for Perth, but we were desperate. We failed there completely. Perth's reputation lingered. She looked immensely relieved. We failed in Cazenovia, too, even with old college friends the Lammes who had bought a beagle from the same kennel where we bought Perth. Perth had an excited reunion with Frederick, bouncing off him and bathing in his saliva as of old, and we spent several nights in our old garage apartment courtesy of the owners, where she sprang off immediately to rediscover the sights, smells and sounds along the lake that for four years had lived only in her memory. But we were deeply worried. We had no idea where we could find a pleasant home for her for the next three months. Someone suggested a kennel but we shuddered at the horror of the idea. We had run out of options and almost out of time. Our plane left Boston for England in a week.

We sat one evening on the little boat pier by the edge of the lake, in a bittersweet mood. This was the very spot where several years earlier as a puppy she had courageously swum after our canoe and we had realised we had a special dog on our hands. The sun was still above the horizon, casting streaks of yellowy silver light across the lake. The water lapped at our feet and Perth in almost a heavenly dream-like state looked out over it. It was almost as if she herself were seeking an answer out there in the dying light. After a while she trotted off silently along the shore.

'Peter,' Cindy whispered to me, 'can't we cancel our plans this summer and just stay here? We would be so divinely happy. Perth, you and I, here in this lovely place where we began our lives together. We could rent our old apartment. Perth would be in bliss. Life would be so easy. Could we do that?'

There was nothing I wanted to do more. No stress or strain. Swimming, boating, romping about with Perth, playing tennis with Cindy, reading, day after sunny day for the whole summer. It would all be so heavenly for Cindy and me. But I thought of my half-completed book, of the crucial additional work I needed to do in English libraries, of the lure of England in general.

'Darling, there's nothing I'd like more than to stay here. I feel the soul of things here, with you and Perth. But if I could just finish the work this summer, we wouldn't need to leave Perth again. If we postpone the trip until next summer, we would face the same problem then, wouldn't we? And I do so want to get this albatross of a book over with. It'll only be three months and then we'll be together again. I'll have my book under my belt and, who knows, on the strength of it we might be able to move to a better university in a more beautiful part of the country. In New England, maybe. Think how Perth would love life there!'

Cindy looked disappointed, but she took a deep breath and said, 'I know, dear, it's difficult. I understand. Don't worry. It will work out right in the end.'

Perth reappeared out of the shadows, preceded by sounds of her paws gently splashing along the water's edge. She looked content, too, ready for anything. We walked silently back to the apartment.

There was a glimmer of hope the next morning. The Lammes had just seen an advertisement in the paper for the Agnes Roy Camp for Girls in Vermont. Why not phone Agnes Roy, the owner, and ask if she would be interested in a bright beagle as a mascot for the girls? The idea was brilliant. The camp seemed tailor-made for Perth, located deep in a pine forest next to a lake in the high country of the Green Mountains. Summer in Vermont is pleasantly warm by day and cool by night. It would be idyllic. She could have the run of the place and the little girls would love her.

'Oh, let's try it,' Cindy shouted. 'What have we got to lose?'

I phoned the camp at once and asked Mrs Roy if she could see her way to taking Perth for the entire summer. I could be forgiven for describing Perth as all good, with no imperfections.

'She is loyal and affectionate, Mrs Roy,' I began. 'She's up for any excursion into the wilds that you take with the girls, and she's no bother at all. She'll walk and run for hours, swim, sail in boats, and make no nuisance of herself begging for food. The girls will adore her. She may even protect them at night by raising an alarm if she hears strange noises outside the cabins. She'll be a comfort to the ones who are homesick, too.'

I held my breath. Bless her heart, Mrs Roy did not say no, but she wanted to meet us and see Perth first. I thought I detected that she liked the novelty of the idea, a camp pet to feature perhaps in the next year's camp newsletter. If the dog proved to be wonderfully affectionate, something for the girls to make a fuss over, Mrs Roy could advertise the camp as a homey and cosy place. For us it was the eleventh hour. If she took a dislike to Perth, we were lost. After travelling to the Green Mountains on a wild goose chase, we would have time left only to find a kennel, somewhere near Boston. Or we would have to leave Perth with Cindy's parents in their apartment and fly off, leaving it to them to find a place for her. They would surely not be too happy about that even in the short run because there were strict rules against pets in their building. Nor did the Prudential Centre like dogs. They fouled up the pavements.

We rushed on to cover the 200 miles from Cazenovia to Vermont, to a village to called Pittsfield on the edge of the mountains. We had never before been to Vermont, and its beauty took our breath away. Lush green meadows spread themselves over the countryside, interspersed with woods and the purest of lakes. Soft, velvet-like, undulating hills and the lofty Green Mountains graced the landscape. There were stone walls as in the English Lake District, which I had not seen anywhere else in America, and the houses were attractive white and yellow wooden-framed and often gabled structures that made us think of witch trials, Nathaniel Hawthorne's *The House of Seven Gables* and an assortment of idealised New England pastimes. In a way, I wish we had been there in the autumn when the colours are raging in the trees, apple cider and maple syrup are flowing, and every other person in the New World woodsman mode is chopping wood for the winter. In mid-June we travelled instead through the richness of summer green. From Pittsfield, we took directions and continued on for about twenty miles, climbing north up into the mountains, through twisting, gravelled, dusty lanes, up and down steep hills and through meadows and woods. We were aiming for a camp near the famous Long Trail, a hiking route that extends from the Appalachian Trail in Massachusetts up into and through the length of the Green Mountains at heights of close to 4,000 feet. It is wild country.

It was exciting but we were nervous. Perth was stirred up that we were on a mission to find her a summer home. She accepted the fact as a result of what her master and mistress needed to do during the summer. And this looked more promising than being cooped up all summer in an air-conditioned house in Florida. So she was straining with her head stretched far out of the window and her front legs hooked over the glass. She sniffed madly and breathed hard. The riot of unfamiliar and delectable smells that passed through her nose almost drove her mad. The road was becoming very bumpy and muddy, with large puddles all along it. We had just begun the final two-mile ascent to the mountain top where the camp was perched. Then suddenly I stopped the car. A real, potentially dangerous problem struck me.

I turned to Cindy. 'What's to stop Perth from coming after us if we leave her at the camp? I think we should do something to prevent her from tracking us, and we should do it now because I wouldn't put it past her to be memorising this route right now.' In my mind's eye I could see her showing up in Boston a few days later. I really did think she was capable of doing this.

Cindy agreed, but neither of us was sure what to do. Then I had an idea. 'Well, we could blindfold her and close the windows so she can't smell anything outside. That might confuse her just enough to deter her.'

'I sometimes think you're as crazy as she is,' Cindy replied. 'But let's do it.'

I had never tried to blindfold a dog before. It wasn't easy because of the shape of Perth's head. She did not mind my doing it, but my handkerchief kept slipping off her ears. I finally managed it by taking a scarf and wrapping it around her head several times, like a massive bandage. She looked as if she had a massive toothache.

'Never mind, Perth, it's just for a few minutes.' She may not have heard me because the scarf entirely covered her ears as well as her eyes.

Pleased with my ingenuity, I drove on. Perth stopped jumping around and breathing hard. She waited and we stopped talking. There was just the sound of the car and birds and the sight of the occasional deer.

As we drove up into the lonely camp, we saw that it was comfortably laid out with several small, neat buildings dotted around. The camp was in a wilderness but not much roughing it went on there. It was a favourite of wealthy parents in New York and Boston who were happy to deliver their daughters from the noxious vapours of the cities to this Vermont paradise for several weeks. It looked well run, in a state of ready anticipation for this year's crop of girls expected in a couple of days. I removed Perth's blindfold and we made for what looked like an office. The three of us walked in. Busy at her desk was Mrs Roy, who was welcoming, but not that welcoming. She did not have much time to spare for us. To our profound relief Perth seemed to pass the test, though Mrs Roy scarcely looked at her. With a wave of her hand she suggested we spend the night with Perth in one of the log cabins and part of the next morning introducing her to the surroundings. She wrote down Cindy's parents' phone number and that was it, all in about ten minutes. One of the counsellors led us to a cabin and we settled in for the evening. After a walk down to the lake, we called it a day and were soon asleep. Perth looked content as she stretched out on Cindy's bed.

The next morning was warm and sunny, a perfect day for Perth to explore her summer home along the large lake and among the trees. The three of us took a canoe out for an hour, then hiked down into a treeless valley, full of wild flowers.

Cindy bubbled with pleasure. 'She'll love it here! In fact, why don't we scrap our trip to England and stay here ourselves as camp counsellors. This paradise is made for us. We'd have a great time.'

'Swap England for Vermont? You've got to be kidding!' I absolutely had to do research in London, but more than that I had a love affair with England going. My father was born in England, my dear aunt still lived there, and I had a hunger for all things English, from its literature, to its lovely old timbered and stone cottages, to its pastoral beauty. On our two previous visits, Cindy had come to love it, too. I even had a passion for English grass, its softness and sweet smell. There is nothing quite like it in America, not even in Vermont. And there are no pestilential bugs in England, no poison ivy or wickedly nasty snakes. It is a benign country. I was not going to be side-tracked in Vermont, though I was delighted for Perth. She would eat this place up.

Then the usual demon of remorse set in. We began to feel terrible about leaving her, even here, for the summer. It began to feel like betrayal again to abandon her for yet another summer, a breach of family faith, a violation of the bond between us. I really did not believe we deserved her. I imagined that by now she must feel unwanted and unloved, that she was thinking she would never leave us like this if the tables were turned. Maybe she was in turmoil inside, pained and dejected. I looked at her looking at me with her large round eyes. What tore at me was that they were so full of love. She would not make a big commotion, but I was sure she was devastated.

At this point, an hour or so before we left, I fell apart and behaved unforgivably. My behaviour would later bring on me an overwhelming sense of guilt and suffering for weeks on end. In my wretchedness, I reasoned that it would be much better for Perth if she did not miss us too much, or even if she did not love us so much. In the hour I had left, therefore, I tried to make her dislike me at the same time as I felt like hugging her. I spoke to her harshly and refused to pet her. I turned away from her. Not even Cindy knew this at the time, but worse yet I pushed her aside with my foot brusquely several times. I was moaning inside as I did it. She was terribly confused and ran around me, trying over and over to get close to me. But I drove her away. We would not see each other again for three months, yet still I was treating her cruelly like this. Perth never whined in her whole life and she did not do so then. But she must have felt like it.

On my instructions, a counsellor held her on a leash as we climbed into the car to leave. She sat down and looked at us quietly as we drove off. The breeze blew through the leaves, the birds sang and life went on. But what had I done? Would Perth hate me for ever? Did I deserve such a dog?

All the way down the mountain, we worried that Perth would follow us back to Boston. We also wondered how she would get on with the girls. She had no experience with children. We convinced ourselves that the beauty of the camp would satisfy her, that she would be safe until our return. The next day we were on the plane heading for England.

Chapter 7

We arrived in London in mid-June and expected to be back with Perth by early September. London was thrilling. Its theatres, concert halls, museums and shops were inexhaustibly nourishing. I immediately got to work in the British Library, burying myself in eighteenth-century books and manuscripts. I was seldom happier than when I was doing that sort of thing. The smell of the ancient pages, the feel of the paper and the handwriting of famous authors all thrilled me. I regularly handled pages touched by John Milton, Alexander Pope, Jonathan Swift, James Boswell, Dr Samuel Johnson and others in the galaxy of English literature. Manuscripts still thrill me after many years of handling them. Occasionally, I hopped on a train to Oxford University to do some reading at the Bodleian Library, in a richly decorated room called the Duke Humfrey's Library which dates back more than five hundred years. Late in the evening, as the room grew darker, only a single light at my desk illumined my world. I imagined I was sitting there in the Middle Ages. I was in bliss and Florida seemed very far away.

On weekends, my godmother and father's sister, Auntie Kath, of whom I was very fond, welcomed us graciously, as she always did, to 'Crossways', her lovely, large nineteenth-century home outside London. Her magical gardens had been written up in several magazines. She ran her household with an elegance, correctness and precision that exuded a delicious sense of well-being. Every Sunday morning we took the train out to her for lunch, where in addition to the best roast beef available on the planet we would often find one of my expatriate uncles from Argentina or Uruguay who was also spending the summer 'at home' in England.

Auntie Kath was the only one of my father's six brothers and sisters who remained in England after World War I. Having grown up in the city of London, where their father was a well-to-do butcher and respected Alderman, in their twenties they were eager to leave the country, thinking the Promised Land lay across the sea somewhere. The eldest sister left for Italy and France, but led by my eldest uncles the rest made their way to Buenos Aires in the early 1920s. In no time at all, my uncles made a fortune in Argentina. My Uncle Harry, the eldest, then invested in about 150,000 acres of the best cattle land in the country, raised prize bulls and built a mansion worthy of the Great Gatsby outside Buenos Aires. One of the wisest things he ever did was to sponsor the invention of the ball point pen by a Hungarian called Biro, from which he made another fortune. My father, who followed them to Argentina in the late 20s, was also a success, but he never made a fortune. I was born there more than a decade later, attended the best British school and spent my summer holidays next to a Uruguayan beach. I did not really live in South America but rather in a British world of South America, a youth of rugby, cricket, polo, teatime, English lawns and gardens, flannel shorts and school ties. The least wise thing my father ever did, after quarrels with Uncle Harry, was to rip me away from this golden boyhood and move to the United States when I was ten. There, absorbed in an American environment of baseball and ugly, heavy bicycles that I never understood, I grew up more roughly, gradually losing my manners and accent, my kinship with my uncles and aunts, and most of all my memories. Only a black photograph album in a Queen Anne desk in our pleasant but unremarkable house outside Chicago reminded me of my extinguished life. Like all immigrants, I was quickly homogenised and pasteurised into American life and culture. I was reinvented with jeans, cowboy guns, basketball and baseball and all the other culturally obliterating elements with which America creates Americans.

America educated me well, however, so I felt confident enough to chase after a Ph.D. More important to me than the degree, though, was English literature, the subject to which I decided to dedicate my life. Through the strong sense of place that illuminates it I was born again into British ways. In my imagination I could live there at last. So when Cindy and I first came to England, I had the strange but pleasing sensation of having been there before. Everything about it seemed natural and comfortable. And Auntie Kath, our family's lone survivor in England who never contemplated leaving it though she easily could have done so for a sumptuous and luxurious life in Argentina, was there to welcome us.

Outside my literary world in the British Library, that first week in London turned out to be a nightmare. One morning in our dingy bed and breakfast lodging north of London – this was our first experience of nylon sheets – the landlady brought us up a letter which had just been delivered from Vermont. The letter spoiled our summer. It was from Mrs Roy. She wrote:

We kept Perth for a few days, but she was obviously unhappy because she kept snapping at the girls. Nobody was actually bitten but it was clear we couldn't keep her any longer. It was just too dangerous. I took her down to a farm about ten miles away where the fourteen-year-old son of the farmer, a friend of ours, agreed to take care of her, feed her and so on. I told him you would pay him when you got back. He had your dog for several days, but two days ago he phoned me to say that she had run away. They looked for her for a couple of hours but there is no sign of her. I'm sure you will understand that they can't keep looking for her. They're very busy on the farm and have more important things to do. The boy, Jonas, said that right from the start the dog tried to bite him. So he had to tie her up on an iron chain in their old barn. He was so scared of her that when he brought her food and water once a day, he had to put on leather gloves because he was afraid she would lunge at him. Every day she got nastier. I don't understand how a little dog like that can frighten a big boy like that so much. I wanted to tell you as soon as I could. I'm sorry to give you such bad news but I've been too busy, too, to look for her. I hope you are having a good time in England.

Sincerely yours, Agnes Roy.

A cold shudder shook us as we read this. We had a horrible feeling of loss and helplessness, of cruelty. Cindy began to cry.

Then I had a surge of confused anger. I was irrationally angry with Mrs Roy that she should take it upon herself to place Perth in the care of a fourteen-year-old boy completely unknown to us. I was also unfairly and bitingly angry with the boy who, it struck me, must surely be clueless about how to care for a dog and ended up being cruel to Perth. But most of all, I was angry with myself. Somehow I must have given Mrs Roy the impression that we did not care that much about Perth, that we were happy to farm her off for a few months just so we could indulge ourselves in a holiday in England. That could have been why she felt she could shift Perth apparently casually to some farmer friends down the road. I imagined with fury how the conversation went between her and her friends when she rang them up about Perth.

'Hello, Bertha, this is Agnes up at the camp. Look, I'm calling because we've got an awkward little problem up here with a dreadful dog that a nutty couple left with us a few days ago. They were on their way to England and dropped her off here for us to deal with over the summer. They called me because someone had told them about our camp, that it was a great place for a dog, and so on. She's a pretty beagle but these people neglected to tell us the fact that the animal is ill-tempered and snaps. The girls are terrified of her.'

'For heaven's sake, that's terrible. Some people can be so unbelievably unfeeling about their dogs. What are you going to do?'

'Bertha, you don't think that Jonas could take her on, do you? He can tie her up somewhere and just be sure to feed her. The owners would pay him when they get back at the end of the summer. He might even take a liking to her, though I doubt it. That dog should be kept away from people, so I thought that on the farm she would be less likely to do anyone serious harm.'

'Well, Jonas could use the money, that's for sure. Okay, Betsy, bring the little terror over. We'll find some place to keep her out back.'

And thus, I told myself furiously, in such a cruel way the die was cast. I exploded.

'This woman tells us about this as if she thinks it will cause us just a little sadness on our lovely holiday! As if we'll quickly get over it. She should have called us before removing Perth to the farm – that's why we gave her Cindy's parents' number. And where does she take Perth? To some farm somewhere where a boy puts her on chains in a dark barn and she sees nobody except him once a day! For heaven's sake, no wonder she became vicious. Leather gloves! What a clot! You would think a farmer would know more about dogs than that. This is terrible.'

Probably the most unforgivable thing I did, to ourselves and Perth, was not tell Mrs Roy that Perth had bitten people before. Here my guilt ran deep, though I could not then admit it to myself. When we were at the camp our backs were against the wall. We were running out of time and had to do something. If I had told Mrs Roy that Perth had nipped people's noses, she would never have accepted her. Anyway, I was convinced that the reason Perth did snap was that Ohio depressed her and she felt severed from the rhythm of natural beauties she had known in Cazenovia. On a mountain-top in Vermont I was convinced her mind and emotions would clear. Her true persona would be restored. What I shoved to the back of my mind were the legions of giggling, screaming girls she would have to endure. The camp was peaceful when we were there. It certainly would not have been once the girls arrived. Perth must have been horrified and unable to control herself. In her position, I probably would have snapped at the girls, too.

My remorse and guilt swept over the brink into tears when I thought back to my own cruelty in the final minutes we were with Perth. Perhaps her misery, the real reason she threatened the girls, fed on her heartache over my harsh words to her, my pushing her aside with my foot. What did she think of me during those lonely, dark hours in the barn? She must have hated me. I felt like one who fails to tell a loved one how much he loves her until it is too late. No wonder she bolted. I imagined her lying battered and bleeding on the side of some road as cars whizzed by inches from her head.

'Oh, she must have pined after us so much, poor dogge, all alone, day after day,' Cindy cried. 'We'll never see her again! We never should have come here and left her alone all that time!'

But what were we going to do now? We tried to call Mrs Roy for more details, but it was impossible to reach her. Then we talked to the airlines about rescheduling our flight so that we could return to Vermont right away and look for her. But the extra cost of returning home was out of the question, far more than our meagre budget would allow. Here we were in mid-June and our return flight was not until late August. There was nothing we could do but wait – and trust that Perth, wherever she had run off to, would have the intelligence and instincts to survive. The genius for finding her way and staying safe that she had shown all her life would now have to serve her as it never had before. We were three thousand miles away, she was in an area of the country completely unknown to her and she knew absolutely nobody to go to for food and shelter. At least it was summer and she did not have to contend with the severe New England winter. We sent up a mighty prayer for her.

Our only comfort in the aftermath of this shock was Auntie Kath. On Sunday we took the train from Waterloo station out to Woking to have lunch at her gorgeous house in Hook Heath, just next to the New Zealand Golf Club. The roast beef dinner she gave us at her elegant table, with her beloved cook Mrs Bostock serving us smilingly as she would at lunches like these for the next twenty years, and with Auntie Kath presiding magisterially and warmly at the head of the table, was balm for our emotional wounds. Over dessert we told her about Perth and that we were thinking of going home.

'That would be silly,' she said simply. 'I know you must be feeling miserable, but you've got work to do, Peter, and you've both made a big effort and spent a lot of money to get here. The pain will ease with time, and I would love to have you here in England with me all summer. Auntie Edna is arriving from Uruguay next week and she'd be most distressed to have missed you. Don't do anything rash. Think about it for a week.'

If we had heard this speech anywhere but in the lovely graciousness of her beautiful house and gardens we might not have listened. Everything there conspired to make us stay – the scent of lavender in the garden, the sun playing festively on the shrubs and trees, the exquisite meal, the comfort of being with my father's favourite sister and the practical good sense that she urged on us. On top of that, I knew I had to finish my work at the British Library. We decided to stay but to keep an eye out for a very cheap flight home, perhaps in late July.

And so the days and weeks passed. We moved out of our dingy flat into a brighter and cleaner studio flat west of London in Bedford Park. We worked in London during the week, taking in plays and concerts in the evenings, and relaxed with my aunt during the weekend. Auntie Edna arrived and for the first time in my life I luxuriated in having with me both my dear aunts at the same time. Cindy loved them both. These were sunny intervals in an otherwise dreary and dejected procession of days.

On one of those Sundays, Auntie Kath made us an offer. She had planned on spending three weeks in Devon, in a small stone cottage belonging to a friend of hers who was away for the summer, but she had to cancel. Would we like to go instead? It would be blissful, she urged. The cottage was next to the ancient parish church in Sidford, up the River Sid five miles from the sea, where the reddish cliffs loom mightily over the coast. It is a walker's and cyclist's paradise. I would have promptly dismissed the idea had I not made rapid strides with my research and discovered several forgotten manuscripts in the Department of Manuscripts at the British Library that tied my whole study together perfectly. I could not believe my luck. In just a few days I felt I could wind things up. So, we accepted my aunt's offer. After weeks of desolation, a few days of escape in a Devon cottage near the sea might just have a healing effect on us. We also keenly desired to taste the soft English countryside, which we still did not know. All I had to do down there for our keep was cut the grass.

I still had not given up the idea of returning to Vermont early to look for Perth, though, and the next day in London, as fate would have it, I stumbled on an extremely cheap flight for one to Boston, leaving in the second week of our time in Devon. On the spot, I decided to take it. Auntie Kath was incredulous and disappointed, but as she often said to me, 'you can't live other people's lives for them'. At least I could spend one week in Devon. I just had to go and look for Perth. In moments of fantasy, I could imagine finding her in the deep forests somewhere. Cindy would stay in Devon the entire three weeks and then return on our scheduled flight at the end of August.

A few days later we were on the train heading south-west.

By mid-afternoon we were installed in the cottage, on the edge of a small green facing the grey stone church in Sidbury. The village was like a picture taken from an enticing coffee-table book: small, thatched, coloured with different shades of plaster and quiet. The rolling hills enveloped us. We hired bicycles and began the next day exploring the area. Every day was sunny and for the entire first week we kept time only by bicycling, doing the rounds of the village shops and chatting with the proprietors and hearing the insistent tolling of the church bells. If life could be better than this, it could only be with the addition of Perth.

Chapter 8

The sun shone brilliantly as I tore myself away from that summer idyll. As I kissed Cindy goodbye on the railway platform that afternoon, the sun seemed to mock me, tempting me to abandon my absurd plan. We had concocted a telephone strategy that would cost us nothing yet keep us in touch day by day. Every night I would call collect from a pay phone in Vermont and ask for Cindy. She would reply to the operator that Cindy was not home, and if I had no good news I would announce to the operator so that Cindy could hear, 'never mind, it's not important'. If I did have news, I would say instead, 'But I must give her some good news. Could you ask when she'll be back?' That would mean that the next time I called, Cindy should accept the call. A transatlantic call in those days cost what seemed like a fortune to us, so if we were to talk to each other there would really have to be some good news.

Reluctantly I stepped on to the train, stayed that night in our little flat in London and caught the morning flight to Boston. Cindy's parents met me at the airport and took me to where I had left our car. They thought I had lost my senses. I barely paused, got in the car and drove out of the city towards Vermont. Just being back gave me hope. Somewhere within two or three hundred miles Perth was still alive. I was sure of it. My plan was to camp since I had all the necessary gear in the car.

My first destination was the infamous farm. By talking to the boy I might get some hint of where Perth may have headed. It was a poor, tumbledown sort of farm sprawled out along the foothills of the Green Mountains. Jonas, the boy, looked so guilty and sheepish that I could not bring myself to get angry with him.

'Yer dog is kinda mean, mister,' he began. 'I didn't wanta tie her up, but shucks, she cut me in my arm one time. My Pa told me to get rid of that damned coon-hound but I wanted to see if she'd treat me better after some days. She stayed mean, though.'

'How did she escape?' I asked him, coldly.

'Yeah, that was kinda scary. I had her tied good and tight with a chain on the post. But if she didn't go and chew right through that big post. Must've dragged the chain with her. You'll never find her now, mister. It's more'n a month ago it happened. She's a gonner. I'm sorry, mister, lemme tell ya.'

I paid the boy what I owed him and left, no wiser about where to begin looking for Perth. Things looked black. Depressed, without much hope, I found a field on a nearby farm and pitched my tent. I shared it with some cows. After a miserable meal in a greasy restaurant down the road, I fell asleep in the tent, exhausted and lonely. Cindy was back in the cottage in pastoral Devon. I was here in a scraggly field in some Vermont backwater, about to start looking for my dog for two weeks, my heart brimming with feelings of remorse over how I had treated her at the girls' camp. I did not know a soul in these parts. The night was full of sounds as I listened from inside the darkness of my tent. There were dogs barking in the distance and some sounded a lot like

Perth. Drowsily, I muttered to myself, trying to rouse myself, 'I must ... I've got to ... get up and see if that's Perth' – but then I sank into a very deep sleep.

The morning light awakened me. I had a greasy breakfast at the same greasy restaurant and then drove into Rutland where I notified the Society for the Prevention of Cruelty to Animals that Perth was missing and bought a large-scale map of about a ten-mile radius around the farm. In order to begin my search I assumed that Perth had not run far, that she had been taken in by some kind people who had a proper knowledge of dogs and with whom she had decided to remain. From past experience when we had temporarily lost her, I knew that she often had the sense to stay put and wait for us to find her instead of wandering all over the place frantically. So I drew on the map concentric, widening circles with the farm as their centre. My plan was to start searching within the first circle and day after day make my way through the outer circles. This way I hoped to cover much of the area methodically. That would be the first week. What to do after that remained to be seen. The problem was that this terrain was not all just open farmland. There was little farmland, in fact. Most of it was thick forest with steep hills and hidden valleys. There were lakes too, and roads that were twisting, confusing and muddy. It was overwhelming, but I told myself that if I started early every morning and kept at it until sunset, I could make progress. I was sure I would find her.

And so I began. My heart leapt into my throat only minutes after driving up into a wooded residential area. I heard a dog barking exactly as Perth did, I mean exactly. Over the years my ears had become perfectly tuned to that sound. The combination of howl and sharp yaps, and their pitch and rhythm, were her trademark. The barking must have been about half a mile away. I turned off the car engine and in the stillness strained my ears towards the sound, which was coming from the trees up the hill, not from the houses below. Sure enough, it had to be her. I leapt out of the car and sprinted in her direction. I closed in on the barking quickly but at first could not see the dog. Finally, after some going around in circles I saw it. I peered hard, trying to bring it into focus. It was a beagle but not Perth. This dog looked remarkably like her, and I wanted her to be Perth more than anything in the world, but it was not her. The complete disappointment and dejection were shattering.

I leaned down to the dog, which was clearly lost and had a damaged leg. 'Well, my little friend, I was hoping you'd be somebody else. What are you doing here making all this noise? You should be at home with your master and mistress. If you've been lost long, I know how they must feel.' I stroked her. She was delirious to see me, licking me up and down. Her collar had her name, Tara, and address. I picked her up and carried her down to the car. She lived five miles to the north, so I drove her there and witnessed the ecstasy of her reunion with her family. They gave me lunch and afterwards I continued on, happy for the family but feeling very sorry for myself.

That first day I moved like a madman. Whenever I was not in the car, I jogged along roads, across meadows, in residential streets, and through thick trees. I never walked. The competitive running I had done in high school and college was finally coming in use. Everywhere I went, I constantly yelled as loudly as I could for Perth. 'Perth', 'here Perth', 'dogge', 'come here, you naughty dog' and anything else I could think of. Perspiring, cut by branches and thorns, wet, I ran and yelled for hours. I was convinced she would hear me and recognise my voice and come bursting out of the trees straight for me. But there was no sign of her. Nothing. Then it was back into the car and the same thing all over again in another area. By nightfall I was a physical wreck. My voice was gone and I was dirty and severely depressed. There seemed little reason to hope. After dinner, I found the tent in the dark and went to bed.

Every day for the next week was the same. Vermont must have lots of lost dogs, for I found five more. But not Perth. And I began to get irritated with people I met. When I knocked at their doors asking if they had seen a dog like Perth, several said 'good luck' but many more said something like, 'Oh, brother, two months your dog's been gone? You'll never find her now, I can tell you that. If she hasn't been killed by a car, there are plenty of dog thieves in these parts who could've picked her up for medical and drug experiments.' On the whole there was little point in defending myself or Perth by explaining that there was no way my dog was about to let dog thieves anywhere near her, or that if she did they probably had paid for their recklessness with a little of their blood. It was easier just to turn away and try the next house. I confess, though, that occasionally when I heard this too often from these smug souls peering suspiciously through their partially opened front doors, I did snap at them with a few crisp sentences. But I also had to admit I did feel that Perth's disappearance for two months now made it seem as if I were trying to rewrite history with a happy ending, like trying to bring back someone from the dead.

My lowest point came at the end of that first week, during one of those long nights in the tent. As my search continued, my feelings of emptiness and loneliness were accentuated; and it was suddenly brought home to me that I was existing in a nervous world of illusion and imaginative self-deception. My life was like a recurring bad dream. Every day I was running through an unknown landscape and among alien people hunting for Perth amid shadows, imagining that random shapes, sounds and places might take me straight to her. I had begun to lose touch with the real world. Even Perth began to seem unreal to me. I was seeing her over and over where she was not.

As it became dark by nine and I could do nothing after that except have dinner and crawl exhausted back into my tent, I decided to escape into another fantasy world by reading a novel by torch light as I lay on my cold and damp mattress. I bought *The Moonstone* by Wilkie Collins, a spooky detective story set in Victorian England, about a stolen diamond and the murder, suicide, sleepwalking, opium and chilling night-time intrigue by moonlight that detective Sergeant Cuff faces when he tries to track the diamond down. It is a long book and there I lay, night after night, in my little tent, vulnerable and oppressed by the frightening quietness of the Vermont landscape, holding the book in one hand and shining the torch light on the page with the other. Except for the light it was pitch dark. The only sounds were my breathing and the turning of the pages.

On this particular night I was in the middle of a chilling passage featuring a troop of mysterious Indian jugglers who appeared to be murderers, when just outside my tent, no more than five feet from my head, I heard a sickening slurping sound, with some scratching and moaning thrown in. My heart almost stopped. I listened in terror, careful not to make a single sound or move an inch. Nobody touched the tent, but the sounds increased. I felt that at any moment I would hear a voice or feel a blow of some kind. This went on for ten minutes before I called on all my courage to switch off the torch. Slowly, I lowered my head on to my pillow. I listened and waited, frozen in fear. The sounds continued, with occasional pauses. Two more hours passed. My courage failed me, to slip out of the tent, for example, and run for it. I perspired in fear. I fought mightily against sleep but eventually it lifted me out of this nightmare.

When the early morning light woke me up, I could scarcely believe I was safe. There was the open book beside me, and the torch beside it. The tent was still up around me, snug and zipped up. There were no more sounds. Unzipping the tent, I poked my head out cautiously and saw nothing except some distant cows. There was no trace of anyone having prowled around in the dark. I walked around to the other side of the tent. There in full view on the ground was something I had completely overlooked before. A salt lick. In my rush, in the dark, I had pitched the tent next to a salt lick! What had terrified me during the night was not a band of bloodthirsty Indian jugglers, nor a dangerous burglar or misfit about to slice through the tent with a dagger, but a few cows licking salt, slurping away in the dead of night.

It was funny, but it was also ridiculous. Was I ridiculous? Was this whole, expensive effort to find Perth ridiculous? Why not give it all up and wait in Boston with Cindy's parents for her return? Even if Perth was alive, it was like searching for an infinitesimal needle in a gigantic Vermont haystack. And she might not be alive, long perished by some desolate roadside. I might be looking for a ghost, chasing a phantom.

At breakfast, I got hold of myself and rededicated myself to the search. I knew Perth was alive. She had to be. I would push on for another week. I now searched a wider area away from the farm, using the map to give some method to my madness. I even drove up high into the mountains several times, yelling Perth's name endlessly into the wilderness and never hearing an answer. I had no idea what she might be doing up there, but that made no difference to me. At one point I found myself on top of Bloodroot Mountain, 3,500 feet up, at another on the banks of the gorgeous Chittenden Reservoir, about ten miles from the farm and surrounded by nothing but the wind and wildness. I still hoped for a miracle, that she would appear from nowhere, baying at me and wagging her tail, and hop in the car nonchalantly as if nothing had happened.

Another week passed with no sign of her. I covered a large expanse of territory. It seemed incredible to me that she could have vanished into thin air. I was sure she ought to have found me since I was all over the place, leaving my scent everywhere. It was unlike her. Nobody called the SPCA, although I left hundreds of people with its phone number and information about Perth.

Deeply dejected, I drove to Boston to pick up Cindy. She was as downcast as I was. But we decided to search for another week together, joined by our Cazenovia friends the Lammes and their own beagle, who sacrificed a week of their lives to help us look. Pitching their tent next to ours, they were encouraging and cheerful, but I could see in their eyes that they thought Perth had perished somewhere. After another week of fruitless searching, we admitted defeat. We had to retreat to Florida to begin the new university term. I had failed. Perth was no more, at least not in our lives. Three months earlier we had left Florida, happy to be on the move, full of hope, and determined to find the perfect place for her where she could be free and safe. Now we were returning with a devastating feeling of incompleteness, that our marriage and family were no longer intact. Except for the first year of our marriage, we had never been without Perth.

It was a dismal trip home, even at Cazenovia where we stopped with the Lammes for a few days. The old, dear Cazenovia scenes of our early married days, where we rollicked with Perth in the innocence of our fresh hopes and family fun, taunted us. One bright morning in particular was painful when we walked for a few miles with our friends and their beagle Tarki. Tarki ran and barked happily, relishing the outing, not with Perth's mad intensity but pleasantly enough. Cindy and I, however, were churned up inside with a sense of loss. Just seeing their dog in the fullness of life and health was more than we could bear. We left Cazenovia that afternoon, not really ever wanting to return.

Chapter 9

But we refused to give up. The first thing I did when I got back home was to make a poster with Perth's picture, explaining where she had run away and when, and most important of all, mentioning that the inside of her left ear was tattooed with the letters PEM. I also offered $100 for her return, no paltry sum in those days. Today that would be equivalent to about $1,000. I cranked out 500 of these on an old mimeograph machine in the English department at the university. Then I walked over to the library and checked out a huge directory of radio stations not only in Vermont but also in New Hampshire, Maine, Massachusetts and Connecticut – throughout all of New England, in fact. That was a measure of my belief in Perth's ability to cover the miles. I wrote a letter to the stations to send with the poster, apologising that I did not have time enough to write a personal letter to each of the 500 stations, and describing my need. The letter went like this:

I should like to ask you the very big favour of announcing on your station as often as you could the fact that my dog is missing, giving something of a description of her, and emphasising the $100 reward. Perhaps most important for final identification purposes is a tattoo inside her ear, which reads 'PEM'. If you could keep the enclosed information on hand as long as one month, giving out the announcement whenever you can, I should be more grateful than I could ever say. Probably a family has the dog in their home, not too clear on how to go about finding the owner, nor knowing that her owners are actively looking for her. Your announcements, if made over a long enough period, may just do the trick.

As I think back on it, how young and naive I was to think that any radio station, busy as they are with thousands of announcements to make every week, would keep repeating my distant cry for help for an entire month. But Cindy and I sealed the 500 envelopes and sent them off, crossed our fingers and waited.

October came and we were still waiting. Our hope seeped with the passing weeks. Many evenings during these weeks I walked into the kitchen and saw Cindy washing the dishes with tears quietly filling her eyes as she dreamed of Perth. To both of us it seemed that without Perth our marriage was changing, or that we were entering a new phase of it without the wide-eyed innocence and adventure the three of us had shared. Our lives seemed tamer. Also depressing was that only one radio station of the 500 wrote back to say they would be happy to help us. And so far as we knew, nobody ever heard any radio station announce anything about Perth. There was only silence from the north.

One bright spot was the manageress of the SPCA in Rutland, a large, jolly woman in her thirties called Alice, who seemed to feel our loss almost as much as we did, and to whom I sent 100 copies of the poster. She wrote back to say she had travelled around to lots of large supermarkets in her area, several of them many miles away, to pin our poster up on their message boards. Without a flicker of doubt, she said we were sure to find Perth. She also went out every weekend to look for her.

October and November passed and we were almost into the Christmas season. There was nothing else we could do, and in an unspoken way we more or less let Perth go. On Thanksgiving Day we attended a church service and heard someone speak whom we usually thought was colossally boring. When he began with the word 'DOG', we pricked up our ears. He went on to say that because a dog is a man's (and woman's) best friend, it is always cared for and protected by people. The dog therefore is perfectly trusting and loving, just as we should be towards God. That was his theme. We forgot everything else about the service except that remark.

'Let's not worry any more,' Cindy said on the way home, placing her hand on mine. 'As the man said, let's just let her go and trust that she is safe and happy wherever she is.' Suddenly we felt liberated from worry, fear and self-pity. Whatever else that boring man had ever said, he was on our wavelength that day.

The next day we took a Thanksgiving break in the Bahamas, for the first time since the summer completely enjoying ourselves without the lingering agony of a lost Perth: swimming, boating, riding bikes, eating out and just loving each other. We returned home on Sunday night, exhausted and purified.

The phone was ringing as we walked through the front door. Cindy answered. It was my father who lived near Palm Beach one hundred miles up the coast. He told Cindy that while we were away he had received a call from Cindy's parents in Boston to say we should expect a precious package on an aeroplane Monday morning. He gave us the flight details. She asked what it was and he then told her, 'Perth has been found!'

Cindy was teaching on Monday morning, so I drove to the West Palm Beach airport to collect the package. I had to go to the cargo department. I signed some papers over a counter, paid a small fee and was led through a door to a small room with several metal tables in it. On each table was a wire cage and in each cage a dog or cat. They were all quiet, numbed by their journey from Boston. For some reason the man left me to find my own cage. I was looking at the papers to see what my number was when all of a sudden there was a huge outpouring of sound from one of the cages, mad, frantic barking, baying and yelping. The moment I heard the vibrations of that voice the world fell away and I was standing again with Cindy outside the kennel near Cazenovia six years earlier listening to Perth as a puppy struggling to escape from her cage and slip into Cindy's arms. I closed my eyes for a few seconds, taking in the delicious sound, then I looked up quickly in the direction of the clamour and saw her immediately in one of the cages. She had spotted me, or caught my scent. I ran over to her and opened the cage. After six months, she was again in my arms.

I forget what I said to her in those first moments, but I remember vividly her soft head against mine and her unmistakable groggy-doggie smell, even after a stifling, dirty flight in the cargo hold of the plane. She looked wonderfully fit. I held her tightly, amazed that after all those months I actually had my Perth again. She was madly excited, as if she were saying to me, 'what happened, why didn't you find me sooner, I looked and looked for you'. She had forgiven me for my cruelty at Agnes Roy's Camp. I let her down on to the floor, grabbed the cage and walked triumphantly out of the building with her. The large car park was full of several hundred cars, but without pausing she sniffed her way to ours. She was waiting by it when I arrived two minutes later. She jumped in, took up her usual position in the front passenger's seat and we were off for home. On the way she crept between my arms and sat on my lap facing the steering wheel, looking out through the windscreen as we drove on. It was like old times, as if nothing had happened. I can still see the round, brown back of her head during that joyful drive. I placed my hand on her white chest and gently rubbed my nose against her. I chattered away to her the whole way. She understood it all, I am sure.

She must have been disappointed not to find Cindy at home, but I told her we would meet her mistress at school in the afternoon. In the meantime, she ran everywhere, over house and garden and neighbourhood, taking it all in. I wanted to take her to the ocean, but I thought we should wait for Cindy.

At three in the afternoon we drove to the school. I stayed in the car and watched while Perth sat waiting on the pavement outside the front entrance of the school, staring at the door for any sign of Cindy. Pupils streamed out, then teachers, but no sign of her. At last she appeared. In a moment Perth was in front of her, front paws on her skirt, her brown eyes riveted on her face. Cindy fell to the ground shouting 'Perth, Perth, Perth', taking her in her arms rolling on to her back as Perth climbed all over her. There they were, the two of them, wrapped up in each other's joy. Our family had been given a new lease of life. We piled into the car and sailed off home for tea. In a couple of hours we were by the ocean, walking on the beach with Perth racing along as in days past, sheer ecstasy in her lungs and the setting golden sun lighting up her body as she streamed along.

Chapter 10

By studying the topography of Vermont and talking to people there, I have been able to piece together what happened to Perth after that fateful day when she ran away from the farm boy with the leather gloves. She got off to a bad start from the first minute after we left her at the camp.

'Perth didn't like it here,' Mrs Roy told me coldly when I saw her at the camp a year later, wagging her finger at me reprovingly like a school headmistress. 'You never should have left her here, knowing that she was so fiercely devoted to you. Your car was hardly out of sight when she snapped at a counsellor who went towards her. Actually, I was surprised she didn't run away, and we did give her a few days to try to settle in, but the girls got frightened of her. I was too busy running this camp to worry about her, too.' Forgetting she wrote in her letter that Perth had not bitten any of the girls, she added, 'when she did bite a camper, she had to go. I'm sorry, Dr Martin, but your dog is not everyone's cup of tea, you know. You should never let her run loose. You'll get sued one of these days.'

I felt like a naughty schoolboy after talking to her, as if I had been found out smuggling biscuits from the refectory. But what we then knew was that my mistreating Perth did not work. She did not love me less because of it. She was even more unhappy being left behind and more determined not to spend the summer there. Thinking back, I could see that in her way she sensed why I treated her that way. She felt it as love. She was not fooled. But she was not sure how to follow us. After all, we had blindfolded her. So, she waited for us to be summoned back for her.

But then she was sentenced to the farm, which was even worse. Tied up all the time in a gloomy barn, seeing nobody except the sullen boy, was torture. She waited, but when she could not take any more she sprang loose, like a coiled spring, determined to track us down, not wait for us to come back for her. She sprinted frantically down the half-mile dirt track out of the farm that led to the forest and the foothills of the Green Mountains. All of Vermont was before her, but she had no idea which way to go. For a week or two she ran, never lost because there was no place she knew, no place called home. The important thing was to keep moving, night and day, not get caught.

She headed north. There were two ways to go. Either she stayed in the low country, along the noisy roads with their traffic, or dived into the forest, climbing up into the mountains where there would be less risk of danger. Knowing Perth, I have no doubt she made for the mountains, where she would have been lucky to find the Long Trail winding its way north, constantly climbing up and down, skirting the Brandon Gap, pushing on by Gillespie Peak at 10,000 feet, and possibly taking refuge for brief periods at places like the Middlebury College Snow Bowl ski centre. Then on north across the Middlebury River, down into the steep and deep Lincoln Gap, and up again the slopes of high peaks like Mt Abraham. At night, when the glory of the mountains had turned to gloom, sleep would have come easily to her, if she was not too hungry.

The Long Trail twists all the way up to the Canadian border, but for some reason Perth stopped in Mt Mansfield State Forest, at a scruffy camp called Campersville poised beautifully on Lake Mansfield among thousands of white birch trees. She had covered seventy miles as the crow flies, but through that terrain and with all her detours to find food it must have been more like 200. She stopped only forty miles short of the Canadian border. Some inner radar had told her not to go any further. Perhaps the nights were getting too cool or she was just too hungry and tired. Or the reason might have been more primitive and instinctual, an unexplainable urge to pause, to wait.

Campersville is a backwater, a cheap place to pitch a tent or hook up a caravan for a weekend. The nearest town, where the owner of the camp lives, is six miles away. There is one simple house in the camp, lived in by Emile Desmond, the manager of the camp, a semi-literate French Canadian. His job was to collect the rubbish, take the money, cut the grass and plough the snow from the road in the winter. He and his wife lived there with their ten-year-old son, Robert. They were very poor. It was there with these people, next to this lake, that Perth decided to cast her bread upon the waters.

She was fortunate. Emile Desmond was a simple man with an uncomplicated heart. He had little to occupy him except his job and he took to Perth right away, who had the run of the house, camp, lake and acres of forest, as well as an endless amount to eat, especially off the grills of unsuspecting campers. He also had a natural way with dogs and knew enough not to force her to do anything she disliked. He neither smothered her with affection nor neglected her. There was no fussing over her, which suited Perth perfectly. He was amazed at how many tricks she could perform and concluded that she was a supremely intelligent dog. When he drove off in his pickup truck to perform his daily duties around the camp, she quickly got in the habit of hopping in to go with him. As the autumn with its gorgeous riot of colour came and passed and winter drew on, they became faithful friends. They were seen everywhere together.

Mr Desmond's son Robert also fell in love with Perth. It was a lonely life at home for the boy with nobody his age to play with, so Perth was his early Christmas present. They slept together at night, explored the lake by day and hiked for miles up into the hills. In the early November snows, Robert hooked up a ragged donkey to a ramshackle sleigh and glided through woodland trails with Perth on the wooden seat next to him staring wide-eyed in all directions.

The family quickly discovered Perth's idiosyncrasies – her vigorous shaking when she dreamed in her sleep, her partiality for the inside of Robert's bed at night, her repertoire of tricks, her adeptness at helping herself to steaks on grills, her love of garbage and her howling when excited, not so much a bark as a long, continuous baying, full of alarm, a siren of emergency. When she did that, her hair rose up along her spine and her muscles tightened like the string on a bow about to be released. The one thing that puzzled them was the strange mark in her ear. At first Mr Desmond thought it was a scar from a wound received in some fight or other; then he made out the letters. But he read them wrongly, as 'PEG', so he always called her that.

The most remarkable thing is that Perth never once snapped at any member of that family. She seemed to under-stand that this now was her home, her safety. Robert had no fear of her. Still, this had not stopped her from snapping at the campers from time to time. She never bit anyone but after a month or so complaints began to come in that she trotted through the campsite at will and, if approached by campers, returned the compliment with a little baring of her teeth and some mild snapping that sent the message, 'keep away'. There was no trouble while the campers complained only to Mr Desmond. He simply warned new campers not to try to touch Perth, and otherwise he ignored the complaints. But sooner or later a camper mentioned this troublesome dog to the red-faced owner of the camp, who had little liking for dogs of any kind and warned Mr Desmond to control her. When the complaints kept coming in, the owner threatened angrily to have Perth taken by the police and killed. He came extremely close to doing that. Emile Desmond had little choice but to stop Perth running freely, except on the other side of the lake from the camp and in the high country. Often he just stuck her in his truck, where she was content. The owner grumbled and dropped the matter.

And so the weeks passed and Thanksgiving approached. All we can do is wonder whether Perth ever gave a thought to Cindy and me, whether she had given up hope of ever seeing us again. Did she dream of us? Northern Vermont, a wilderness around her, warmth and enough food, and love – were they enough to erase the memory of her first six years with us? Or was she waiting, still hoping, for the sound of our voices, our sharp yell in the air, 'Here, Perth!', with the cutting accent on 'here'? How many times had she imagined she heard that? When she went into town with Mr Desmond, did her eyes dart around longingly and expectantly, trying to spot us? Would a female voice resembling Cindy's suddenly light her up? Would a tall figure like mine make her look up hopefully at a stranger's head to see if it could be me?

One mid-November day in town, an older friend of Mr Desmond's shuffled up to him, pipe in mouth.

'Hey, old friend, about that dog o' yours,' he said, looking around for Perth, who was back at the camp. 'You seen the poster in the supermarket? It's about a lost dog. It's been up there for a spell now. The picture of the dog looks a dead ringer for that beagle you got, the stray you picked up. You seen in the dog's left ear? Something about a tattoo of PEM. Kinda odd. Anyway, the owners are giving a $100 reward for her. You think you've got their dog? You oughta take a peek in that ear. Christmas is coming. A hundred bucks ain't no joke.'

'Nah, it couldn't be. We had the dog a long time. Where is the poster, anyway?' They walked into the IGA supermarket to take a look.

'Well, will ya look at that,' Mr Desmond whispered when he saw Perth's picture on the poster. 'It sure is 'er spittin' image. But all beagles look like that, don't they?'

'You'd be rich.'

'My dog has a tattoo but it says PEG, not PEM. I don't wanna get rid of the dog, anyway. My boy'd be sad.'

'All the same, better look in her ear again. A hundred bucks is a hundred bucks. You can't turn yer nose up at that, man. Christmas is coming on.'

When he got home, Mr Desmond made straight for Perth and looked in her ear. The tattoo was faded but sure enough, it said PEM. His spirits sank. There were no two ways about it. Peg was actually called Pem and she belonged to someone else, someone who painfully missed her and was willing to give $100 for her return. But he was not going to part with her. He loved her, and so did his son. This dog was his now. If he had not saved her, she would be dead now. Anyway, she was happy with them. He would say nothing to anyone but his wife.

But in the next few days he got to thinking about Christmas and how that $100 would come in useful for presents. The boy wanted so many things. His wife was also on to him to get rid of the dog and get the money. Then his conscience began to worry him. Peg was not his dog by rights. Her owners must be miserable without her. If a dear dog of his own were lost, he would be furious if the people who found her refused to return her to him even when they knew who he was and how to reach him. He was torn apart, not knowing what to do. If only Perth could tell him what she wanted.

He saw her lying in a patch of sunlight on the porch. It was one of those sumptuous Indian summer Vermont November days. She was warm and happy. Her eyes were half-closed in enjoyment. He sat by her on the porch floor and stroked her sun-warmed coat. She opened her eyes, raising her head slightly and looking at him.

'Peg, old hound, I wish you could understand me and tell me what you think. I know who yer owners be and they want you back with 'em, but they don't know you're here. You wanna stay here, old friend, or you wanna go back? What d'ye think, eh?' He spoke softly. It was like talking to himself. Perth put her head back down on the floor. But she did not close her eyes. There was something in the tone of his voice perhaps that stirred her.

Mr Desmond agonised about what to do and finally, after talking about it to his son, decided to give Perth up. He told his son it was the right thing to do. She was not really their dog. Also, they would have lots more money for Christmas. The boy cried and hugged Perth. That afternoon he and his father went into town to call the number of the SPCA in

Rutland, which I had put on the poster. He spoke to Alice, the woman who had helped me so much to try to find Perth over the months. She was jubilant.

'Oh,' she shouted, 'Mr and Mrs Martin will be dancing up and down the streets. They've been looking for Perth for months and months. What wonderful news. Thank you, Mr Desmond, for calling.'

'Her name's Peg, not Perth,' he said on the phone. 'Or maybe Pem.'

'Peg? No, no, Mr Desmond, it's Perth. PEM are Mr Martin's initials. He tattooed them in her ear six years ago when he bought her.'

'Six years old! She don't look like six, more like two. She's a great dog. My son and I don't want to give 'er away to nobody. But we sort o' need the money.'

'Yes, of course, I understand. It must be very difficult for you. Now, tell me where you live and I'll come over to see you in the morning.'

'No, I'll come there.' He knew that if he gave her his address, there would be no turning back. He was still unsure he would give Perth up when it came down to it. He would see when he got there and spoke to the woman.

Early the next morning he drove the sixty miles down to Rutland with Perth on the seat next to him. Alice was waiting for him in her chaotic office. He left Perth in the truck and walked in.

'How do you do, Mr Desmond, thank you for coming all this way. This must be very difficult for you. Let me tell you, I'm so excited to see Perth. But where is she?' She was all smiles.

He was glum and careful. 'She's in the truck, but what I wanna know first if the owners really do love 'er. I won't give 'er up otherwise. Maybe they forgot about 'er by now.

'Mr Desmond, I've never known two people who love a dog as much as the Martins love Perth. You've got to believe me. They've never given up hope of finding her. They call me every week to see if there's any news about her. Do you know, when they first lost her they came from England especially to look for her? Mr Martin spent three weeks hunting for her, doing nothing else.'

'If they loved 'er that much, why they didn't take 'er with 'em?'

'It wasn't practical for three months. They had to be in London.'

He seemed satisfied with the explanation. Reluctantly, he got up. 'Well, I better get the dog, then.' In a minute he was back in the office, Perth standing beside him looking at Alice.

Alice stared at Perth as if she were seeing a legendary animal, scarcely able to believe she was real. So this was the little dog who had caused so much misery and trouble, who had run across the state of Vermont and survived for six months. This was the dog who had terrified a campful of girls in the Green Mountains and compelled a teenage farmer boy to wear leather gloves, the dog who had been cruelly tied up in a barn. She was struck instantly by how beautiful this beagle was, how lean and fit.

'Hello, Perth,' she said softly. 'I'm glad to finally meet you.'

Perth cocked her head slightly. She had not heard her name mentioned for six months. It was a sound from the past. She wagged her tail slowly. Alice approached her.

'Take care,' said Mr Desmond, 'she might bite you.' Alice knew this about Perth, though, and was not about to take liberties with her.

'It's okay, I'll be careful.' Then she tried an experiment. 'Where's Peter, Perth, where's Peter?'

At that, Perth burst into life. She wagged her tail vigorously, barking sharply and running around the office excitedly, sniffing everywhere for some sign of me. Here was a woman who knew both her master's name and her own. Her master must be near. Where was he?

'Oh, this is Perth, all right!' Alice shouted. 'Peter's coming, Peter's coming, Perth,' she said. Alice crouched down and Perth walked right up to her, placing her legs on her arms and looking up eagerly at her face.

Watching this, Mr Desmond knew he had to let the dog go. But he needed the money and would not give her up until he had it.

'Will you leave Perth here, Mr Desmond? I'll call the Martins and break the good news. They'll send you the $100 right away, I'm sure.'

'Oh, no, my boy's gotta see 'er again. She'll come back with me. You tell the owner to come pick 'er up at my place.'

'They live in Florida, so that might be difficult. You can trust them, Mr Desmond. They're honest folks. If they say they'll give you the money, they will.'

'No, I've gotta take 'er back. I'll tell you how to get to my camp and you can bring 'em.'

'Okay, thanks. We'll work something out. It was very good of you to come.'

He gave her the directions. Alice hugged Perth before they walked out. 'Don't worry, Perth,' she said. 'Peter's coming.'

Alice had Cindy's parents' number in Boston and wasted no time calling them. We were in the Bahamas and could not be reached, they said, but without hesitation they said they would travel the 200 miles up to Vermont on the weekend to pick Perth up and pay the reward. They would drive to Alice's SPCA and then go on from there.

That week the Indian summer ended. A violent snow blizzard hit New England, covering most of the region with a foot of powdery snow, which was great for the big ski industry in that part of the world but awful for anyone trying to find a tiny camp in a backwater of Vermont reachable only by dirt roads. Few of these roads were marked on the map and scarcely any of them would be snow-ploughed that weekend. The Peters, nervous but thrilled to be playing a major part in the great drama of the Return of Perth, arrived at Alice's early Saturday morning. They set off immediately to give themselves plenty of time, Alice in her truck, Cindy's parents in their car. Once they arrived in the areas of the mountain ski resorts and approached Mt Mansfield State Forest, they hit a maze of snowy roads and got lost several times. It was treacherous driving. Miraculously, they found the camp before the sun had set.

Father, mother, son and Perth were waiting in the draughty, cold house. What had looked like a lakeside paradise in the lovely autumn now looked like a lonely, dark spot at the end of the earth. There was a feeling of melancholy about the place. Alice went in while the Peters waited outside for everyone to come out. When they did, followed by Perth, there was a great commotion. Perth was all over them in an instant.

Standing in the driveway, they got down to business. Robert held Perth, dejectedly, and said nothing. Mr Desmond told them everything that had happened: how Perth had arrived, how they had fallen in love with her and her spirited ways, how she was almost put to sleep by the blustery owner of the camp, how they found the poster, and how he and his son did not want to let her go. Cindy's father gave him a cheque for $100 and thanked him profusely for saving Perth. He told them about us, where Perth had run away from, how we had looked for her for three weeks in August, and that it had been for us like losing a child. I think it must have made the lonely father and son feel better about giving her up. Then Alice pulled a surprise out of her car, a little six-month-old abandoned beagle puppy. She handed the puppy to Robert, who cradled her in his arms.

'Robert,' she said to him, 'this isn't Perth, but it's a beagle and it looks like her. You must take good care of her the way you did Perth and love her for many years to come.' The boy was overjoyed. He took the puppy into the house, then came out and gave Perth a huge hug. His father was sadder and took a longer time over saying goodbye to Perth. It was obvious that Perth loved him very much. But when Cindy's mother opened the door, Perth hopped in straight away and sat there on the big rear leather seat, waiting with quiet dignity, as if she knew exactly where she was going. Alice, the heroine of this struggle, hugged the Peters and then they were off.

They drove non-stop through the snowy landscape straight to downtown Boston, into the car park below their towering apartment block in the Prudential Center. From there they warily took Perth in the lift up to their flat on the twentieth floor – nervously because dogs were absolutely prohibited anywhere in the building. Perth was quietly confident the whole way. In the space of a few short hours she had been lifted out of an obscure camp in the backwoods of Vermont into the heart of one of the most cosmopolitan, affluent, modern city environments in the world.

As she walked through the door of the flat, instead of the bare wooden floor planks of Emile Desmond's house, which she had grown to love, she stepped onto plush wall-to-wall carpeting that spread itself across the rooms like a smooth lawn. She trod upon it curiously, in and out of rooms, fascinated as she might have been by a magic carpet. It seemed to never end. Instead of rough plywood walls with murky window panes looking out on fluttering birch leaves and mighty conifers, all around her were immaculate white plastered walls with huge plate glass windows through which, by jumping up on a chair, she gazed out on the cityscape of Boston, with its tall skyscrapers and canyon streets far below. In the distance was Massachusetts Bay. On the other side of the flat still more panoramic windows let in views of the distant landscape outside the city, in the direction of Vermont. Instead of rickety chairs with torn fabric and white stuffing popping out, she sat like the Queen of Sheba's honorary palace pet on broad armchairs with plumped-up, immaculate cushions, smelling of strange, fine fabric. The beds were like football fields. She could climb under the covers of one of them and never come into contact with anyone else in there. Had she awakened from a dream or fallen into one?

The next day, while Cindy's father bustled about arranging for her to be flown to Florida in a portable kennel, Perth stayed in the flat and waited. They ventured out only twice, risking discovery in the lift as they descended for walks on the teeming pavements below. By nightfall, everything was prepared for her return, and early the next morning before dark they took the lift to the car park in the basement. Then into the car for the drive to the airport. In the cargo department, the Peters hugged her and she walked unhesitatingly into her cage, without a flicker of protest. Nobody can doubt that she knew who would be at the other end of the flight. The Peters watched from the departure lounge as the plane with its treasured cargo rose gracefully into the sky.

Chapter 11

Perth had made her break for freedom in Vermont and survived. It was time for us to make our break from Florida, but when and to where remained to be seen. Reunited with her after months of painful separation, we knew only that a new beginning was in the air.

Florida's ocean still thrilled the three of us and we made good use of it. It continued to amaze us that so many Floridians, including people who had recently taken up residence in the state, turned their noses up at the tourists from the north. They called them 'snow birds' because they fled from the snow down to the sun and ocean. Smugly, the thin-blooded residents avoided the ocean, thinking it beneath them to do such a 'touristy' thing as swim in it. It was much too cold, they said, too rough. You must be mad, they told us, to swim in it in December. But we thought the madness was theirs and we swam with undiminishing pleasure. Existence in Florida never seemed richer than when the three of us cavorted on the beach, Perth disappearing into the bush while Cindy and I rode the waves in the frothy surf. We could do it for hours.

Even with the ocean and sunshine, however, there seemed little reason for us to stay on in Florida. It was dull. After her misadventures in the mysterious Vermont hinterland, Perth also thought it was stale. Except for her hunting sessions through the palmetto scrub and secret gardens of the idle rich, she had nothing to do. Life seemed to be passing us by. An ocean of events during the turbulent late 60s had come and gone, but down in the land of milk and honey we had felt scarcely a ripple. Before us spread an enervating world of lotus blossoms, a land of forgetfulness and stagnation. We all had to get out.

Another summer rolled up soon enough. We had rented a stone cottage up on the rocky Maine coast and were aching to get there. This would be the summer of all summers, with no travel, no pressing research, no bed and breakfasts, no anxiety of separation. Just wild seagulls screaming over the North Atlantic, the waves crashing against the rocks, the brightest sunshine in the clearest air imaginable, red lobster beckoning to be eaten on the rocks with melted butter, lots of swimming, delicious cool evenings by the surf, saltwater taffy to eat – it was a northern paradise. We would watch the passing of the hours and days without stress or worry. It would be Perth's new frontier. She would explore unfettered. Catching the excitement of our talk and preparations, she was impatient to be off, breathing hard, restless, her eyes wider open than usual. This was more like it. We might all get lost up there and never find our way back to Florida.

We aimed the car north and shot up along the east coast, churning up the terrain along the shortest and fastest route I could find. We wanted to enter that cottage and stay there. Nothing would distract us. We stopped in Boston only long enough to pick up Cindy's parents who were spending the first week with us. They had a long love affair with Maine and, having rescued Perth from Vermont and forged their bond with her, they wanted to spend some time with her too.

When we arrived, Perth immediately disappeared into the

coastal landscape and for the first few days we scarcely saw her. The cottage was perfect rusticity and picturesqueness. We all relaxed. Nobody told anyone else what to do or not to do. This was how it went for about a week; then suddenly I had to drive south to Boston to see somebody. I stayed overnight in Cindy's parents' apartment.

I was brushing my teeth the next morning when the phone rang. It was an English voice from a college in England. I had met the man the previous summer.

'Dr Martin, are you still interested in teaching here?' he asked. 'We have a sudden vacancy in our department that we'd like to ask you to fill.' I took the toothbrush out of my mouth and tried to compose myself and say something coherent. 'The only thing is, we need to decide on your appointment very quickly,' he added.

'Yes, I am definitely still interested,' I replied, trying to sound as matter-of fact as I could. 'How did you ever find my number here?'

'We had it in our files. We tried your number in Florida first. Is it, then, an offer you'd like to accept?'

'Must I answer that at this precise moment? Could I ring you back in a couple of hours? My wife is in Maine and of course I need to discuss it with her first.' I almost added that I needed to consult my dog as well. Images of Perth racing across England's green and pleasant land pleasingly flickered in my mind.

'Call me in a couple of days,' he answered.

He hung up and immediately I rang Maine and spoke to Cindy.

'You'd better sit down to hear this, I began. 'I just got a call from southern England, Sussex to be exact. They offered me a job, to begin this October. What do you think?'

For a few seconds there was silence. Then she caught her breath and shouted 'yippee'. In the twinkling of an eye we decided to accept. I rang England back and in a few seconds I had secured a teaching position in my father's native land, the country that through its literature I knew best. I lived in America but for years my imagination had dwelled in England. Now my body as well as my soul would live there. By the time I put down the phone I was already transported out of my corporeal American existence into a land of dreams. The world around me suddenly changed, imbued with a glow of hope and anticipation. Everything seemed better, lighter, charged with promise.

Was this offer of an English lectureship going to launch an expatriate chapter in our lives? It could well be, I thought. I knew at least that I was eager to leave America. So was Cindy. The problem was that although we were fond of Americans and their bold optimism that anything is possible, we thought the lifestyle in the country had changed dramatically in the 60s and was showing signs of getting worse. It was not so much the growing distrust of authority and tradition, which was showing itself most acutely in universities, but the accelerating 'dumbing down' of culture in so many ways. America has always been a land of exaggeration, with Americans proud of all things being bigger, better, faster and easier. Their ingenuity has never been in question, but it seemed to me that often the only reason one could come up with to explain something new was simply the national fascination with novelty. If it can be done, do it, even if there is no need for it, even if it damages the existing nuances of life. As long as people buy it or flock to it, as long as it makes money, it becomes a virtue. I shivered at the mass culture that was raising its hydra head more aggressively than ever. Since I taught students about language, encouraging them to see its precious and delicate beauties, neither did I fancy the abuse of English that was gathering momentum in that cradle of commercialism. Language seemed to be merely the hand-maiden of moneymaking, effortlessly and smilingly violated. Say or write it any way you want to, especially if it can perpetuate mass culture. Bend it out of shape. It was all oppressive and demoralising. I realised much of my unhappiness originated in my own mind, but that did not help much.

So, when this offer to live in England landed in our laps, we snatched it up hungrily, eager to be gone. There was lots to do. We had to rent our house but we could not afford to drive back to Florida to arrange it. That would have to be done by post and phone. We could also get by in England with what we had packed for a summer. As for my job in Florida, a quick call to the university and I had secured a leave of absence for two years.

The main problem was Perth. After the initial euphoria, it hit us that sending her across the Atlantic was not that straightforward. The paper work, shots, airline arrangements and transport cage were trouble enough, but where would we send her? And on that point our naivety came painfully face to face with harsh reality.

'You can't fly with your dog on the same flight,' the British consulate in New York told us on the phone. 'In fact, you won't be permitted to pick her up at London airport. You won't even be allowed to see her.'

'I beg your pardon,' I replied limply. 'Why not?'

'Haven't you heard of British quarantine laws?'

Embarrassed, I admitted I had not. 'What are they?'

'No dog – and I mean no dog, not even the Queen's, if

she had a foreign dog – is allowed into Britain just like that. Any dog brought in from another country has to spend six months quarantined in an approved kennel on British soil, a kennel designated for that purpose. And you have to pay for it, I'm afraid.'

'You've got to be kidding!'

'That's the law. The reason for it is to keep rabies out of the United Kingdom. The UK is the only part of Europe without rabies, and the government wants to keep it that way. There are absolutely no exceptions. I can help you make the arrangements, if you like, to place your dog in a kennel near where you'll be living. All quarantine kennels more or less cost the same. But in light of this information, you may just want to leave your dog in America, give her to friends or family. We advise it, in fact. It's better for the dog.'

I felt like clubbing him. 'But why six months, for heaven's sake? I can't put my dog in a kennel for six months!'

'Exactly. I recommend leaving her here. You can get a nice dog in England and, believe me, your dog will be much happier here than in a kennel. And think of the money you'll save. It'll cost you about forty pounds (about sixty dollars) per month to quarantine her, not to mention the cost of shipping her over.'

I hung up. Since leaving Perth behind was out of the question, we had some hard thinking to do. Should we take this job, after all? On top of everything else, an expense like this would play havoc with our finances. My salary in England was going to be less than in Florida anyway. In our more pessimistic moments, this is what the picture looked like: we would be leaving a nice home in subtropical Florida with all modern conveniences, a good salary and a life in which Perth played a major part, in order to take a job at a lower salary and live in rented accommodation in a cold and wet environment where we would be forcefully separated from our beloved dog, paying dearly for the privilege besides. Not only that, she would have to live in a cold prison, surrounded by cement and wire. Cruel, selfish, and foolish, surely that is what we would be if we went ahead.

That was the bleak view. We had to think ahead. We could probably survive the expense of quarantine, and then what would we have? After six months of hell, Perth would be free to run in England. She would have before her the pastoral green fields, meadows, hills and gardens of bucolic Sussex instead of the sterile and constricted mansion gardens along the Florida beach. There would be endless wildlife she could track, chase and howl at. We would certainly have a garden with a lovely, soft lawn on which she could lie. We would all be together at last, permanently, with no need to be separated in the summer, for it seemed impossible that we would ever return to hot America during the vacation. And Cindy and I would lap it all up as much as Perth would, walking on the picturesque South Downs, taking tea in the garden, appreciating the greenness of the landscape throughout the year and enjoying a culture that was more congenial. All around us would be the world that I studied, taught and wrote about. Surely six months of hardship were worth it.

I remember on one of those windy last days in Maine, alone with Perth on the rocky coast with the roar of waves beating angrily around us, asking her what we should do. We had our ways of communicating. I told her gravely, in a falling, confidential voice that it meant six months of imprisonment for her. She shook the spectre off. She looked beautiful. Her eyes and briskness of movement spoke of adventure, going forward, taking risks, not looking back. The briny water sparkled on her brown head, which she held high into the wind. I knew we had to go.

Chapter 12

Since at this point Cindy had even fewer doubts about moving to England than I did, we set about robustly making arrangements. The main thing was the kennel to which Perth was to be sent. The closest one to the small market town of Arundel where I would be teaching was in Alton, Hampshire, a drive of about ninety minutes. Quarantine kennels were few and far between. One or two that were closer were all booked up.

'What does it matter how far the kennel is from where you live?' I remember the nasty man from the consulate saying to me. 'You'll probably rarely see her anyway. Dog owners like you come in here all the time moaning about how cruel the system is, how they must have their dogs with them in Britain, how they'll visit their dogs every week in quarantine, and so on. And then they end up seldom making the effort to see them. The dogs are the real sufferers.' Maybe he was right in general, I thought, but he could not speak for us.

Once her place in the kennel was arranged, we booked her on a flight in August. The consulate man was right, we quickly discovered. We could not fly on the same plane as her. So one Monday morning we drove her to Logan airport in Boston and assigned her to the cargo department, far away from the main passenger terminals. Perth looked chipper and ready to get into her cage, trusting us. We were not as happy as she was, though, because we knew she was headed for another cage in England. Nor were we sure when we would see her again. Our flight was the following week. We hugged her, rubbed our heads against hers, smelled her clean beagle smell again, and walked away. She made no sound as we left.

Her flight was straight to Heathrow airport, London, where she was kept in her cage until picked up later in the day by an employee from the kennel in Alton. He slid the cage with her in it into the rear of his white van, having seen to the considerable official paperwork. Perth did not set foot on English soil until she was released from that cage into her larger cage at the kennel. But there was no soil even there, of course. Just a cement floor. She saw no trees and smelled no flowers. She was handled like a convicted criminal who is taken directly from the courtroom to prison. And the kennel shared a feature with a prison in that it was completely surrounded by eight-foot concrete walls.

Her confusion must have been profound. Instead of being greeted by us at the airport and taken to a comfortable home where she could begin her new life of discovery in England's soft greenness, she found herself lying quietly on a cold cement floor in a cage next to many other cages containing howling, yapping, snarling, defiant dogs of all descriptions. It was bedlam. She had never known anything like it. Where were her master and mistress? It would only be a matter of time before we came to deliver her from this hell, she must have thought. But night came, and then the morning after, and there was no sign of us.

We were still in Boston, waiting for our flight in a few days, unaware of her caged hardship. When we thought of a long-term kennel in England, we pictured a type of dog hotel, not a high-security animal prison. So except for the dismal thought that Perth would be in the kennel for six months,

103

we did not imagine or brood over how she would be treated. The irony did occur to me, though, that a year earlier we had been stuck in England miserable over Perth's disappearance in the Vermont hinterland; now we were stuck in Boston and she was incarcerated in England, heaven only knew where. Every imagined paradise has its disfigured underbelly and Perth had found one of England's in a matter of an hour.

Our day finally arrived. We boarded the aeroplane and headed for the Old World, which for us was the Brave New World. Eight hours later we were in London. Four hours after that we were in West Sussex, fifty miles south of London. Luckily, in a newspaper I bought at the airport, I saw an advertisement for a modern cottage in the little village of Bury, not far from Arundel, available immediately. We also saw an old Volkswagen beetle parked outside the airport with a 'For Sale' sign on the windscreen. A Dutch hippie, frayed around the edges, was leaning against it. After a little nego- tiation, we bought it from him – he clutched at the money – piled our bags in, and made straight for Bury.

The cottage was perfect, modern yet tasteful and pic- turesque with a small garden and the greenest grass. I looked in the garage and found countless garden tools, types I had never laid eyes on before. And the village was gorgeous, the quintessence of village Englishness, a picture from a storybook. Twelve hours of travel had exhausted us, but we unloaded our baggage, pulled out the map, found Alton on it, hopped in our beetle and headed west. That August in England was beautifully dry and warm, and the winding route to Hampshire we traced across the countryside on such a flawless sunny afternoon took our breath away. Everything was so neat, picturesque, so green, so clean.

'How exciting,' Cindy exulted. 'Here we are in England,

the perfect expatriates, travelling across this heavenly landscape, about to see Perth!' For people who had romanticised about it for years, the landscape was all we could have wished for. One after another the sumptuously luscious fields followed each other in an endless succession of glorious images. Stone walls, trim hedgerows – those were the days when farmers and county councils were more assiduous in trimming and protecting them – neat roadsides, charming thatched and tiled stone cottages, picturesque copses, rolling common land, the occasional country house set in its extensive ancient paternal acres and deliciously inviting pubs created scenes that were obviously nurtured by a society that treasured its countryside. This landscape was unmistakably loved. It was an extension of English identity, all laid out on a human scale without the severe encroachments of commercial billboards and without offensive housing developments, raised by rapacious money-makers at every turn. And it was so accessible. You could easily walk through it. Seductive footpaths abounded on every side.

We had no idea what to expect at the kennel. The place was set among some beech trees just off the road. The first thing we noticed was the incredible noise of the dogs, a fury of panic and frenzy. In the small office we found a man who confirmed that Perth had arrived and that we could see her straightaway since fortunately we had arrived during the afternoon visiting hours. He led us through a corridor outside into a large and cold cement square or yard surrounded by the eight-foot stone walls. The only piece of furniture in the yard was a single wooden bench. There was green moss and algae on the floor and walls where the sun's rays never reached. The stench of dog excrement was overpowering. This was the high-security receiving area where people could

105

be reunited with their beloved pets. It was not a place where you wanted to linger, however, even with your dog. In fact, the man told us later that owners did not come often to see their dogs, if they came at all. So far, we were the only visitors that day.

We wanted to come with the man to see where Perth was, but he stopped us. 'Government regulations, I'm afraid,' he said. We waited while he fetched her. We both felt distinctly glum. Neither of us spoke. All that we could have said was written on our faces. Ten minutes later he reappeared through a green door with Perth on a leash. Without ceremony, he took it off her and disappeared.

She looked up, saw us and flashed across the yard to the bench where we were sitting, howling in frantic excitement. As she often did when she was keenly excited, like on the frozen lake in Cazenovia, she did not immediately jump into our arms but ran in circles around us several times and up and down the yard, in a frenzy of delight. Then in this desolate space we embraced each other for the first time in England. Her warm and smooth body felt reassuringly familiar. Surprisingly, she looked fit and smelled clean, with even a little of the groggy-doggie about her.

'Dear dogge,' Cindy mumbled in her ear. 'Are you okay, are they treating you well? We miss you so much.' I massaged her shoulder muscles and pressed her head against mine. Her eyes were bright and wide open with understanding and excitement. After a while, she stretched herself out on Cindy's lap, happy just to feel her warmth and comfort. We told her about our cottage, Bury, the garden and the beautiful world that spread itself out all around the village. We talked on and on, and she listened.

'It'll be wonderful, dogge, when we're all together in our

cottage,' Cindy said. 'You'll love it. Plenty of rabbits and lots of hills to explore. We need to be patient. Before you know it we'll be taking long, fresh walks together.' We gave her a few titbits to eat. The minutes ticked away, many of them silently as we lost ourselves in thought.

The man reappeared at four to ask us to leave. Perth allowed him to put the leash on her.

'Don't despair, Perth, we're all in this together,' I said to her strongly, as the man tugged at her urgently. 'Eat your food and when they give you a chance to exercise, run like mad all around. Keep fit.'

We squeezed her and then the man walked off with her through the green door back towards the howling cacophony of cages. Just before she was out of sight, she turned and took one last look at us. We left, dejected and worn out. We would not be allowed to see her again for a month.

Chapter 13

Our gloom even survived the picturesque drive back to Bury, but we had lots to do at home and we set about it briskly. In the days that followed the nagging thoughts of Perth's misery and the month of forced separation from her cast a lingering shadow in the sunshine of our new habitation. But we had to look around us and begin our new lives. We discovered the village, our fellow villagers and the endless footpaths through meadows and hills and along the River Arun that glides gracefully past the village down by St John the Baptist parish church. The word got around that some 'Americans' had moved into the village, and before long several long-time residents were dropping by to say hello. It is unique to an English village that once you have settled into it you may feel you have been there for ages, that you have had dreams about it, that in a mysterious way it is your natural and predestined home. It is like an ancient myth of memory and tradition that recurs so often in the imagination and becomes so familiar as an idea of human need and reassurance that you recognise it instantly. You put it on as naturally as you do an old shirt or coat. It makes you feel like yourself.

The typical English village of course is both ancient and very much part of the real world. In its ideal, unspoiled state it is complete and independent, a beautiful and fruitful place to live. You scarcely need to step out of it, except to work perhaps, as I had to in nearby Arundel. Bury is still like that. It has its own church, school, pub, shop, post office, farm (where we can buy milk, cream and eggs) and kennel. It also has an array of societies and clubs like the horticultural society, toddlers' play group, music appreciation society, tennis club, ramblers' or hikers' organisation, cooking club, cycling club and the Women's Institute. And the village governs itself with a Parish Council that tries to make everyone happy with a minimum of controversy. The Council also strives to fight off hostile 'townie' money-makers who cruise in to buy this or that cottage or piece of land for renovation and development and in the process threaten to destroy the very ancient village myths and traditions from which they think they can make money. In recent years that has been like trying to plug up multiplying leaks in a crumbling dyke.

Cindy and I quickly detected in Bury another presence that people who do not live in a village can easily miss, an impalpable aura of safety and protection hanging in the air. More than just a sanctuary or retreat, its place in the landscape exuded permanency. Embraced by nature, it was in tune with its cycles and seasons as it had been for centuries. It was a sense of security that neither of us had ever had before. I understood for the first time an essence in the literature of England, what writers from Chaucer to Shakespeare, Jane Austen, John Keats, Kenneth Grahame and the great poets of the last hundred years have described and celebrated: the deep sympathy and affection the English feel for their landscape and how they use it to explain themselves to themselves.

Bury is fortunate. It sits silently at the feet of the South Downs, a wide, expansive, rolling stretch of hills eighty miles long where almost nobody except farmers live. To the east the village unfolds down a slope of meadows and fields of barley and wheat towards the river, beyond which stretch water meadows and the green Downs beyond. Like a perfect stage set, in the distance Amberley village with its medieval castle is perched harmoniously in the middle of the picture. To the west a little lane winds through a series of sequestered villages and hamlets, all silently tucked under the Downs. Along this lane footpaths lead off either up into the hills or into the adjacent pastures. In the village itself the thatched and tiled cottages are strung sociably along the two lanes that intersect it, so that from the gardens of most the surrounding countryside is open to view. In a minute, footpaths from any part of the village lead you into the freedom of the open landscape.

All in all, it was a paradise made for us and Perth, clouded for the moment with the melancholy fact that she could not enjoy it for six months. But the weeks passed quickly and around midday one Saturday a month later we were beating the path to the kennel again, the dark spot in our imagination. When we arrived, we were ushered unceremoniously into the cement yard where we waited for Perth. The smell was no better than on our first visit. The minutes ticked away and then there she was at the door. The man unhooked her from the leash, her head darted up, she saw us on the bench and in a second she was all over us.

'What a wonderful dogge,' Cindy shouted as she wrapped her arms around Perth on her lap. 'Have you been all right all these weeks, without us? Do you think about us? We miss you terribly, sweet, courageous Perth.'

Still not one for licking anyone wildly with a flapping tongue, not even us, Perth showed her emotions by looking straight into our eyes with the deepest and most loving look, breathing heavily. She stepped back and forth between my lap and Cindy's, occasionally letting out a howl. The tenseness in her body gradually dissolved and after a few minutes she settled down on Cindy's lap. None of us said much, but there was no need to speak.

Seeing her there, strong and still beautiful, I realised how much we had missed her. We sat for a half hour without stirring. My eyes travelled dejectedly over the lifeless, cold, uncompromising cement enclosing the yard. 'Five more months of this, Perth – can you take it?' I whispered as I stroked her head and back, massaging her shoulders. Then my eyes fixed on the eight-foot walls on the other side of the yard from the main building. I could see the tops of the tall pines beyond it. On the other side of the wall was open common land, miles of it, with no roads or people. A dog could lose herself in it. I sprang to my feet, grabbed Perth off Cindy's lap, and carried her to the wall.

'Run like mad, Perth, and don't come back here!' With that, I put my hands under her chest and stomach and with all my strength threw her up towards the top of the wall. If she could just clear the eight feet, she would fall outside the compound and could make her escape through the trees, shrubs, and ferns. We could then later drive the car down the road, double back by foot, and look for her. It would be easy to find her.

But I could not throw her quite high enough. Her front legs reached the top of the wall, but the rest of her body dragged her down again and she fell onto the hard cement, unhurt and rather excited. Howling at me, she wanted me to try again. I was about to when Cindy ran over and grabbed my arms.

'Are you mad? Do you want to wind up in prison, too?'

111

she said desperately. 'What would you tell the man when he came back to fetch Perth? How could you explain why she wasn't here?'

'I could tell him anything. I could tell him that a man we didn't recognise had come in to take her back to the cage. Or we could simply tell the man in the front office that she was still in the yard and make a hasty exit.'

'But they'd track us down in Bury and find her. Then where would we be? In real trouble, that's where. She'd have to start her six months all over again. Or worse yet, they might put her to sleep, put her down. Don't be insane!'

I was about to argue that we could hide her, that after several weeks they'd give up looking for her. I was sure I could throw her over the next time. But then the fit passed and I walked back to the bench, defeated. Perth and Cindy followed. We quietened down and Cindy reached into her basket, pulling out a large lamb bone from last Sunday's lunch. Perth took it gingerly and began to rip the meat off it over by the wall, taking time and doing it thoroughly. Her teeth had had no real exercise for a month. It was strangely satisfying to watch her do it, a kind of primitive and instinctive act that made her seem more part of existence.

Perth was still at the bone when we left a couple of hours later and finished it off, splinters and all, in a day or two. 'Be brave, dogge,' Cindy said. 'We'll be back next Saturday morning.' Perth looked at us with feeling, telling us she knew we had tried to free her, that we felt as miserable as she did. Without fail, every week after that – for now we could visit her any time we wished – we returned and re-enacted this ritual of quiet commiseration. I never tried again to throw Perth over the wall. One bright spot was that the kennel hired

112

a young woman called Allison, who took an immediate liking to Perth and tried to make her life easier. Several times she joined us on the rigid bench in the yard.

Another bright spot was that after three long months we heard of another quarantine kennel with a vacancy in the village of Elsted just ten miles from Bury. We rushed there to inspect it, for anything would be better than where she was; and since the new kennel was so close to home we would be able to visit her at least twice a week. When we saw the kennel we knew Perth had to be there. Elsted village is in an even more remote and rural setting than Bury, away from any major roads and at the end of a winding lane that stops at the Downs. The kennel itself is flanked by the Downs on one side and surrounded by rolling common land. Instead of traffic, there were only the sounds of birds, sheep, cows and a distant rooster. Occasionally a horse trotted by on a bridle path. It was also a smaller kennel with a staff who understood the hardships that the owners of the animals suffered and did all they could to make life more pleasant for them.

We made the arrangement to have Perth transferred immediately, and within the week, one day in late November, she was brought to Elsted in a high-security van with bars on the rear window. We were not there when she arrived but we saw her the next day. The front office was clean and well-lit and several pleasant young girls were bouncing around cheerfully seeing to this and that. One of them took us to Perth's cage, which we had never been allowed to see at the other kennel. There she was, beneath a heat lamp, lying on a floor covering that kept away the cold of the cement floor. The cage was spacious, fifteen feet long, though narrow. And luxury of luxuries, there was piped-in music. There were also fewer dogs and little noise. Three times a day they took her out to an exercise yard where she could breathe some fresh air. She looked tired but happier.

'Perth, we're here,' I yelled when I saw her in the cage. She howled her hello. 'Hold on, dogge, hold on. We're going out to the yard. They'll bring you there.' We hurried to the yard, a fenced grassy area five times the size of the walled cement prison-like yard in which we had spent so many hours. Through the fence you could see the hills and ferns, rabbits, birds playing in the bushes and (if you were lucky) an occasional deer.

'I feel like I'm in a garden,' I said gleefully to Cindy.

'It's so much better and so close to home. We could dash out here every day if we had the time!'

Perth joined us in a few minutes and we spent some joyful romping time with her that first morning in her new home. She was transported, sprinting on the smooth grass up and down the length of the enclosure. Always a sign of her happiness, she rolled over and over on the grass, rubbing into her coat its purities and refreshment. She howled at the rabbits and sniffed the wind off the Downs.

It was very cold so we did not stay more than an hour, but we were there long enough for us to get another inspiration. Standing by the cage saying goodbye to Perth, I said, 'Let's buy a really comfortable, stuffed armchair for her to curl up in. You know, with fat arms and a thick cushion. I think the cage is wide enough for us to squeeze it in. I don't think they'd mind. The cold months are coming on.'

'Genius. A great idea. It would be a lovely Christmas present for her. What do you think, Perth, would you like an armchair like that one you chewed up in Ohio?'

Apparently nobody had ever suggested such a thing before,

but the manageress thought about it and saw no problems, provided we could squeeze the chair in. We went straight out and bought one from a second-hand furniture shop in nearby Petworth. With some shoving and pounding, we managed to cram it tightly into the cage just under the heat lamp. Perth jumped up on it instantly, curling up against one of the arms on the soft cushion. Beneath the benign warmth of the heat lamp, she closed her eyes. It was the most comfort she had felt in more than three months.

That winter was one of the most severe in southern England for a decade. The ground hardened before Christmas, the hare 'limped trembling through the frozen grass', and ramblers decided it was too frigid even for them to wander over the icy landscape. There was no heating in the kennel except for the heat lamps, and the cold floors were painful for the dogs. Perth was lucky. We brought in a couple of blankets for her which, with the heat lamp, kept her cosy in her armchair. The armchair eventually became legendary in the kennel. Many years later at a university in America we ran into a girl who long after Perth's time at the kennel had become a kennel maid there. When we mentioned the chair to her, her mouth fell open, her eyes widened and the blood rose to her face. The chair was still there, she said, gasping. It had been used by generations of dogs in that particular cage. Since it was so tightly squeezed into the space, nobody had bothered to try to get it out. Hundreds of dogs had been grateful for it even during the time she worked there. It was Perth's comforting legacy to countless dogs in that part of southern England.

For the next three months, several times per week we saw Perth at Elsted. She kept warm and we all felt as close to each other as we could in the circumstances. But secretly it was misery to us that she was not sharing our reincarnation in England, our growth into the pleasures of village life and the secrets of grove and green. From almost the start of our marriage, we had shared everything with her – except England. The grass had been wonderfully green all this winter, as it always is in England, but now it was growing again with the rising sap, smelling sweet and lush, while she languished in her cage. The snowdrops had come and gone, as had the crocuses and primroses. Now the daffodils were making their bold appearance and new-born lambs were frisking in the pastures. Much of the time during our visits with Perth she had her nose raised into the air, catching rousing scents of the earth that carried primeval messages. The breezes also brought sounds that she translated for herself. She knew what was going on out there in the coppices, by the trails up the Downs and along the streams that flowed down from them. Nature was stirring. At night there were less familiar sounds, haunting and appealing. But there was nothing for her to do but wait and dream the fantasies that were shaping in her mind.

Then one warm morning in March the triumphant day arrived. Perth had served her time and earned her freedom. Waking up trembling with excitement at six that Saturday morning, far too early since the kennel did not open until ten, we decided to drive there and wait by the entrance for three hours. We walked up and down in front of the entrance, waving to the kennel maids arriving for work who by then were all our good friends. They were almost as excited as we were.

'This is Perth's big day!' one shouted as she strode in. 'And yours, too!' she added. There was still more than an hour to go before they opened up, so we started up a footpath that climbed the Downs. About three hundred feet up we emerged above the tree line, into the open, and were able to look down on the village and the kennel. The folds of the bluish hills stretched to the east and west. I decided to send Perth a message from above. In the old, familiar cry – the one I hurled at the Vermont wilderness thousands of times when I was looking for her – I shouted as loudly as I could in the direction of the kennel, 'Here, Perth, we're coming'. After a few shouts, back came her answer, a rapid explosion of barks and hounds. 'That's right, dogge, coming, coming,' I yelled. She kept up her replies. I think she knew her time had come. With that we made our way down quickly and arrived at the kennel just as it was opening.

With a kennel maid we made straight for the kennel to let her out. 'Perth, you're out, you're with us now, forever,' Cindy blurted out. Perth was calm, on her best behaviour as if she were afraid they might put her back in the cage if she erupted too soon. In the office, we signed the papers, thanked the kennel maids who gathered around and were each in turn hugging Perth goodbye, and walked out with Perth most definitely *not* on a leash. She hopped into the car and we drove off.

About a mile up the lane, I stopped beside a large stretch of beautiful common land decked out with ferns, gorse, riots of springtime flowers and woodland. I opened the door. All I said was, 'Time to run, Perth! Go!' We knew what she would do. She took a quick look at us and out she sprang. Almost before she touched the soft green turf her legs were pumping furiously. She sped off across the springy ground, heading nowhere in particular, just raging to stretch her legs and infuse her whole being with the physicality of the natural world. She was out of sight in seconds, but her yapping and howling as she tracked a paradise of new scents reached us for a long time afterwards. Her sounds could be heard downwind from a couple of miles away. Over the next two hours as we sat in the car, we heard her giving the chase in the hills, in the deep reforestation of conifers, in the thick brown bracken surrounding a system of dew ponds in adjacent National Trust land – she was everywhere, it seemed. Then for long stretches we heard nothing. We waited.

'She's free at last,' Cindy said, 'the first time she has run loose in England. It must seem like a magic land to her.'

'Now life in England begins, for all of us.' I glanced at my watch. 'If she ever comes back, that is.' Perth was seven years old, in the prime of her life. I felt I knew her as no other man could ever know his dog. She had to cleanse herself, get rid of six months of kennel smells. Whatever she was doing out there, it was her own instinctual form of communion with the spirits and genius of the landscape. It was her baptism. Our job was to trust her, and wait.

There was neither sight nor sound of her for hours. We had taken our own walks and napped on the grass and bracken. The afternoon was wearing on and we were anxious to get home for tea. It was getting dark. Still, we waited. At about five I looked out of the window of the car and suddenly there she was. I said nothing at first. I had never seen her looking so tired. She was caked in mud, scratched by brambles and thorns and covered by all manner of clinging vegetation. She could barely hold herself up but her eyes looked up to mine with a contentment we had not seen since Cazenovia days.

'Good dog,' was all Cindy said as I opened the door and Perth jumped wearily on to her lap. We drove off through the green twilight to Bury.

Chapter 14

It was not long before Bury villagers noticed that something had been added to the village, and they were not sure they liked it. As in Cazenovia, we could not bring ourselves to tie Perth up for any reason, at any time. We were nervous that this might damage our new friendships, but we felt we had no choice. It would be a breach of trust with Perth to put her on a rope. It would break the vow we swore to each other the day we bought her. More than that, though, we would be forcing her to be a different kind of dog. And what kind of reward would this be for her after six months behind bars? Part of the joy of moving to England was the thought of her running all over it. There we were in Bury surrounded by fields, hedgerows and hills teeming with all sorts of wildlife. She must be allowed to know it. But most of the villagers had dogs that they strictly controlled. One hardly ever saw a dog running loose. The only times, in fact, one saw dogs was when their owners walked them in the lanes and footpaths. We would have to see what happened.

On the Sunday morning after we brought Perth home, we drove up Bignor Hill, at the top of the chalky Downs, about seven hundred feet up. The lane takes you through several tiny villages and hamlets, turns left in Bignor at the Roman villa, and then continues steeply up a gravelled track. As we climbed, Perth stretched her neck out of the window, straining to allow scents and other messages from the woods to pass through her twitching nostrils. She began to breathe heavily, almost frantically. I was reminded of the fateful day we blindfolded her on our way up that Vermont mountain to Agnes Roy Camp. This was a brighter, happier day. We were all together and we were going to stay that way. Her eyes were flashing and wide open. It was all we could do to keep her from jumping out.

Halfway up we let her out and immediately she disappeared into the tangle of thicket. Not long afterwards the silence was broken by a pounding of hoofs and Perth's howls. Suddenly a deer shot out across the lane, followed by a rabbit a few yards behind and then Perth chasing both of them. They vanished just as quickly. Rather than wait for her we went on to the top where we parked and walked for several miles on a section of the Roman road from Chichester to London. Perth was nowhere in sight when we got back to the car, so we made our way down slowly, yelling for her as we usually did. Halfway down, out she leapt across the lane in front of us, followed by presumably the same rabbit and then presumably the same deer chasing them.

She rejoined us a few minutes later at the bottom. 'What was all that about, you hound?' I asked her. She looked at me as if I should have known. It was a mystery we never solved, but it seemed an appropriately eccentric and symbolic start to her life in England. Who knew what went on out of our sight, in the tangled hideaways of those hills where for years to come she would scout and chase. We started hundreds of walks with her that we never finished together. She had a life of her own up there. She could easily run a hundred miles over a weekend. As far as we knew, she never caught a rabbit or harmed any other animal. Did she find mysterious, magical places where animals meet each other on equal terms, not hunting or hiding from each other? Was it these places that swallowed her up for hours on end? One thing was clear: Perth had found her Garden of Eden. Life could get no better than this.

As it turned out, the villagers did not worry about Perth as much as we thought they would. She trotted friskily into their gardens, but she never fouled them up or did any damage. Occasionally she howled her away across them after a rabbit, but gardeners are happy to have anything chase rabbits out of their gardens, or even kill them. Also, most of the time she preferred the open landscape of field and pasture. She could be gone a whole day. Many days she was content simply to stay in our garden and sun herself, stretched out on the grass. So she did not become infamous in Bury. People came to accept her as a fact of life, like one of the local village characters, of which Bury had many back then.

This is not to say there was not the occasional blow-up. One of the local teenagers, David Bream, the son of a carpenter who had lived his whole life in the village as his ancestors had for generations, and one of the local pub's lager-louts who was drunk as often as not, one day happened to be in the wrong place at the wrong time. Or maybe it was Perth who was in the wrong place. There was something about him, his hot temper perhaps, that infuriated her. If she saw him in the lane she would take on the character of a wild dog and go at him with a frightening howl, the hair on her back standing on end. She would always stop short, sliding to a halt about five feet from him, but not before she had sobered him up a good deal and taken a few years off his life. Here was a bad seed, she must have felt. Nobody else ever provoked her this way. He did not deserve her hostility but she thought he did.

Normally he swore at her in his native Sussex brogue and stumbled on. One summer morning, however, when I was in the front garden weeding while Perth was basking in the sunshine with her eyes half shut, he came sullenly by our front gate. He was perfectly sober and in no mood for pleasantries. He did not see us, but Perth saw him. She exploded, howling, bristling and stretching her neck as she lunged towards him. My heart missed a few beats. There was no time to call her back, not that it would have done any good. She pulled up short as usual but kept up her furious racket.

This time he had had enough. He grabbed a rock and with a torrent of foul language heaved it at her. He missed and only made her more furious.

'You mongrel bitch, shut your bloody mouth or I'll take your head off.' He grabbed two more rocks as Perth danced around him tauntingly. He threw them both and missed again. This gave me time finally to act. I loudly called Perth off and she retreated.

'You bad dog!' I yelled at her. 'Go back in the garden and I'll deal with you later.'

But I had seen enough to anger me. I had never seen anyone throw something at Perth. It was like someone throwing a rock at me. I stormed up to him. Staring into his face, I boomed, 'You must be crazy, man. You could've killed her. If I were you, I'd think twice before you throw anything at my dog again!'

He looked at me threateningly. It was not until this moment that I noticed he was very big. The Black Dog and Duck pub, I later found out, used him as a 'bouncer', whose job it was to throw out anybody who had drunk too much and was a disturbance. His neck was massive, and though I was taller his limbs were a lot thicker than mine with muscles. I sensed danger and backed off. He glowered at me for a few seconds, then turned and walked down the lane.

A few seconds later he turned on his heels and shouted, 'You ought to keep that bloody dog on a lead,' muttering a few more things I could not hear as he shook his fist at me.

'Perth, you can't do that sort of thing here,' I said to her harshly back in the garden, 'not if you want to be happy and free. Get hold of yourself and leave him alone.'

She looked at me, cowering, afraid I was going to strike her. She may never have heard me so angry at her before. She understood and never bothered David Bream again. The experience was an important moment in her life. After that, on the lanes and out among the public, as far as I know she never threatened anyone again. Nobody ever complained. I put it down to her survival instinct. She knew when to pull back from danger. Like that line on the road in Cazenovia that I had taught her not to cross for her own protection, this fracas on our quiet lane in Bury taught her not to step over into danger. Unless, that is, she felt enclosed or restricted. If that happened, to our cost we would discover again that she was unpredictable.

Chapter 15

David Bream was not, in fact, a bad seed, but he was something of a black sheep in an ancient Bury family that within
memory had always existed on the frayed edges of the com-
munity. All villages have had such marginal characters, the
ones the villagers gossip over and like to malign, or exclude
from the sociability of the village geography of cottages, lanes,
village greens, pubs and shops. There is something medieval
in the identification of such people as troublemakers, scape-
goats, the rotten apples in the barrel of half-conscious com-
munity superstitions. In the Bury village I have known they
have never been deliberately shut out, but there they remain
on the edges. And Perth's radar somehow picked up on the
grudge against David Bream's ancient lineage.

The David Breams of English villages are regrettably an
endangered species. They are victims of the forces of pros-
perity, mobility and overpopulation. As people with money
from towns and cities have bought their little pieces of rural
bliss in villages, gobbling up and renovating ancient cottage
after cottage, too often with little idea of living in the village
except at weekends during the summer, middle-class dullness
has replaced the memories and traditions of the old, native
families who with taxes and other costs cannot afford to
continue to live in their family homes. They wind up literally
on the fringes of the village, in soulless modern council houses

and other dwellings, replaced by commuters and the like who have not a clue about the village's past. Nor do many of the newcomers care a fig about several hundred years of village history. Coming from the States, it was precisely the ancient character of Bury, and of countless other villages like it, that tugged at our imagination so powerfully. It was a shock for us to discover that there were many people who wanted pieces of Bury chiefly as a recreational escape from London, or as an investment, or for a suburban-type existence. They can have their drinks parties, neglect the traditional village shop by driving to the nearest supermarket for the week's groceries and respectably keep the parish church going, but many seem blithely oblivious to the rich traditions that resonate throughout lane, cottage, field and river.

Perth, if you think about it, was tuned into that resonating past in Bury more than most. She knew nothing of modern affluence. All she cared about was the landscape embracing the village as it had existed for generations. She knew the layout of the village better than anyone except the disappearing old-timers. From her travels in and around the village she felt the antique rhythms of the place, the effects of the seasons on the land, the movements of animals, the sounds of everything. She could even detect in David Bream a perturbed spirit from the past, dislocated and virtually uprooted in the present.

No wonder it is, then, that such native villagers often walked around with chips on their shoulders. They were losing their world. You could find them sequestered in evenings at the Black Dog and Duck, whiling away the hours in chatter. I grew to appreciate David over the years, and he actually came to be fond of Perth.

There were other natives who were still in the village when

we began our lives there but who have since died or moved. When the writer John Galsworthy carried on a squire's existence in Bury in the 1920s, writing his famous books on the top floor of a large rambling country house next to the village shop, he assembled a retinue of servants, gardeners and chauffeurs, most of whose families had lived in the village for generations. Galsworthy died forty years before we arrived in Bury, but his servants were still there, willing to reminisce.

Then there were the old village cricketers, like Frank Barnett, for decades the village postman who made his deliveries by bicycle, logging many miles over the hilly countryside. He was a great batsman and could have played for the county had he had the money. He was one of those grumbling locals who never fitted in, even into the old ways that have now vanished. We liked him, though, and he loved Perth. He never minded her sniffing around his large vegetable patch. He was eighty-five when we first met him. His wife was seriously ill and they were childless. He dwelled in one of the loveliest of the old flint, thatched cottages across the lane from the parish church, seven hundred years old in fact, but he lived in poverty, subsisting mostly on the huge number of potatoes, leeks and carrots he grew every summer.

When his wife died several months after we got to know him, the lawyers informed him that over the last fifty years she had secretly salted away in the local bank huge sums of money. He was suddenly rich. One of the first things he did with his new-found wealth was take a holiday in Blackpool. He also bought a refrigerator and strip lighting for his kitchen. Otherwise, his money disappeared among his nieces and nephews.

It seems Frank Barnett did not entirely trust his wife because for decades he himself had tucked away in his garden shed hundreds of gold sovereigns of mint condition in little leather pouches. Many of them dated from the late nineteenth century. When Cindy, Perth and I were sitting with him in his dingy kitchen one day after his wife's death, he pulled out one of these pouches and gave a sovereign to each of us. We still have Perth's. It is a talisman.

He stroked Perth and said, 'That'll remember me to ye. The wife could ne'er abide dogs. Never had 'un.' 'Don't ye spend it all sudden-like,' he told her. She leaned against his leg affectionately.

He died the following year and was buried beside a towering yew tree in the churchyard across the lane, but not before I interviewed him about Bury history and got it all on tape. In the background you can hear Perth howling loudly at something while Frank speaks in his gravelly, hollowish, almost inaudible tones, so that on the tape she seems to be transfigured into an ageless Bury phantom merged with Frank's chronicle, a disembodied howl from the past.

Two or three of those old Bury families struggle on in Bury today but nobody pays them much attention. They are part of the village's threatened collective memory. On a brighter note, however, the village, confronted with the rapidly receding traces of its history, is now at the eleventh hour stepping up to preserve whatever light on the past it can before it vanishes forever.

Chapter 16

Imperceptibly, Cindy and I grew towards the decision to spend the rest of our lives in England. She luxuriated in the glow of English rural pastimes and village life, and Perth had claimed her own widening territory as a type of divine right. Perth's world now ranged from the village to include miles along the top of the Downs, innumerable commons scattered about in the hilly ground at the feet of the Downs and several farms and villages. She went wherever she wished, whenever she wished, often returning haggard, ragged and scratched. Once she arrived home with her belly hugely swollen and dragging on the ground. An adder – England's only poisonous snake – had bitten her in one of those sandy, scrubby commons, but this was only a temporary interruption. The swelling disappeared in a couple of days and then she was off running again. The only part of the landscape without any appeal to her was the coastal plain south of the Downs.

In the spring and summer of our second year, two major events occurred, both affecting Perth as much as Cindy and me. Cindy was pregnant and in August would give birth to a boy named Andrew. And because of that, we decided to move from our rented cottage to one at the upper end of the village, opposite the Black Dog and Duck, where we live to this day. We bought it for a song because it needed a lot of work, but it was a dream, from the start almost mythical in our imagination.

We were told that Appletree Cottage was four hundred years old, but it turned out to be almost six hundred. It was built as a peasant's manor cottage, connected with the eleventh-century Bury Manor down by the river. Constructed with the mellow, honey-coloured greensand stone that lies eighteen inches below ground in that part of the village, it was originally a medieval open-hall cottage. Its interior was simply a single large room reaching up to crude rafters on top of which a pile of thatch was laid and tied. The peasants who lived in it in the fifteenth century lit their fires in the centre of the room and allowed the smoke to blow out between the rafters and walls. It was their hearth. They cooked over it and sat around it with their children as, late into the evening, the dying embers, cast shadows on the rough-hewn, unplastered walls. They bedded down for the night on the dirt floor, near the fire. As often as not, they shared the space with various animals, not only companionable pets like Perth but chicken, geese, sheep and other farmyard beasts. It was a rough, dark, cold, hungry, smelly life, not the idyllic rural existence often portrayed in English literature and painting. And much of the time the family was exhausted down to the marrow of their bones.

Some time in the sixteenth century a beamed ceiling was introduced into the room, creating two bedrooms upstairs separated with some massive beams unmistakably taken from some derelict ship's timbers. At the same time, a chimney was built at the end of the building with a large inglenook downstairs to go with it, a fireplace supported by another huge eight-foot wooden beam that stretches across the top of it. Hundreds of years of nails and spikes embedded in the

129

antique wood are still visible. The inglenook is large enough to accommodate two or three people in it to cook, bake bread, or just sit. There is a brick-lined oven carved out of the thick walls to the side. With these improvements, therefore, life for our ancient predecessors in the cottage was suddenly warmer and more private. In the seventeenth century another section was added on to the end of the house, a room downstairs and one upstairs. The cottage stayed that way until the twentieth century, when after World War II a tiled wing was added on to the back for a kitchen and bathroom.

Seen from the lane, the cottage with its lovely stone walls and heavy covering of thatched reed screamed to us to buy it. But the view from the front did not prepare us for what was at the back. On the first day we went up to speak to Mrs Holmes about buying the place, it took my breath away when I walked around the side of the cottage into the one-acre garden. The garden was magical but the view was visionary, poetic. On the other side of the two hundred feet of hedge and riot of daffodils along the edge of the garden unfolded fields after fields of springing wheat and barley, knitted together by endless hedgerows and falling away north and east down to the River Arun. Past the river were wild wetlands, overlooking which was perched the romantic, fairytale twelfth-century Amberley Castle, the equal of anything you could find in Tuscany. And farther in the distance were the Downs and thick woodland. Perth, Cindy and I were joined in a revelation as our eyes travelled over the complex beauty of hundreds of acres across a panorama of 180 degrees. Man, woman and dog felt the influence of spring. Cindy's arm swept the horizon gracefully. It seemed that the whole earth lay before us, a gift from God. It was as if we had dropped down from heaven. It was a final resting place. The garden was our terrace, the stage from which we looked out on the world. There was no going back.

My first thought was, 'Perth can trot on out through that gap in the hedge and never have to stop for anything, not for roads, cars, houses or people.' It was like a huge landscape garden, an endless playground for her of green, mist and sparkling waters. She could come and go in perfect safety. Just as I was thinking that, Perth pushed her way through the hedge and into the fields. She stopped and quietly looked out to the horizon as she took in the view and the lay of the land. She then turned to us as if to say, 'You must buy this. I want to live the rest of my life here.' Then she lay down in the sun on the grass, her head turned towards the view.

We walked into the cottage to speak to Mrs Holmes. She was eighty-five and the cottage reeked vilely of fish that she was cooking for her cat. The carpets were threadbare, the walls needed plastering, it was cold and damp, and the kitchen was in a miserable state. The stairway to the bedroom upstairs was like a ladder. The cottage was so bleak that when Auntie Kath came down from Surrey and saw it a few weeks after we had bought it, she said urgently, 'I think you'd better cut your losses and sell it'. The bathroom was shabby. Its crowning features were an old discoloured bathtub and a toilet that seemed at odds with the human anatomy. One flushed it with one of those old chains pulled from above.

But the old part of the house was unspoiled and unchanged, as it had been for hundreds of years. It was like a time capsule. Since it was built, nearly six hundred years of human history had passed. Shakespeare had written his plays. The Italian Renaissance had come and gone. Genghis Khan and Peter the Great had created empires and passed into oblivion. Many cataclysmic wars had been fought in which millions were butchered. Within those thick stone walls, however, virtually nothing had happened. Only humble people with humble histories had lived and died there. Nobody had told their stories and nobody ever will. Except for a thick meat hook on one of the beams, stains in the woodwork and a few bent iron spikes where centuries of clothes and other possessions had hung, there was nothing to tell us about their hopes, defeats, victories, tragedies, loves and hates. The ill-lit rooms were, as the poet Keats put it, witnesses of 'silence and slow time'. Only the residents' ghosts remained to make us wonder how many acts of violence, murders, beatings and infanticide may have occurred there; how many lovers embraced there; how many children dreamed of the infinite world outside the murky windows as they were dangled on their elders' knees.

'You came just in time,' Mrs Holmes said. 'I was about to write to the actor Richard Widmark to offer Appletree Cottage to him. He's wanted it for years, ever since he acted part of a film here. But if you want it you can have it.' She had taken a liking to us.

She named a price and we accepted on the spot. Two months later we had moved in. She moved to the nearby town of Arundel while we began plastering, painting, cementing the floors, laying out carpets, putting in a new stairway, repairing the plumbing and electricity and improving the heating. Otherwise, we did nothing to change the structure and feeling of the place. We saw ourselves as temporary caretakers in the long saga of its life. It became a way of life. Everyone has a dream home in mind. Appletree Cottage was our waking dream.

There was also a good omen. As the cottage is at the upper

end of the village, for centuries its inhabitants have drawn their water from an eighty-foot deep village well just on the other side of the hedge, next to Bury Hollow, the deep lane over which the cottage hangs somewhat precariously. The well was a major engineering project when it was dug and lined with stone several hundred years ago. All villagers had the right to use it. At the turn of the twentieth century, however, when water was piped into most of the cottages at that top end of the village, the well fell into disuse, although the seven feet of water eighty feet down remained as pure as ever and could have supplied the whole village even then. But there is an ancient statute that if no villager used the well for twenty-nine years it could be enclosed within the boundaries of the nearest cottage, Appletree Cottage, and become a permanent part of that property. And that is what happened, so that when we bought it the well had long been inside our hedge.

The problem was that the owners of the cottage had neglected the well and allowed the wooden well sweep to rot and disappear. Nobody had told us about the well, and we failed even to notice it when we moved in because it was concealed by vegetation. There was barely a sign of it on the ground except for several pieces of perishing wood that covered its opening, four feet across. These planks would not support a dog, much less a person who had the ill luck to stray into the vegetation and tread on it.

From the first hour we moved in, of course, Perth had been sticking her nose into everything, so she must have stepped on to this rotten wood several times. Nothing happened, but surely eventually she would have fallen in and drowned if a shy farmer down the lane who had grown up in the village, as had several generations of his family before him, had not secretly stolen into the front garden in the dead of night. Without telling us, he replaced the rotten wood with a thick plank of sound oak. He has a deep well on his farm, too, and later we discovered that ten years earlier his son had fallen into it and been killed. The moment he heard that a new family was moving in he took it upon himself to cover our well. He also cleared away the growth, exposing the well to full view. We saw it the next morning and knew that some village genie had done this. The farmer, who later became a dear friend, was thinking of children we might have, not Perth. But it was Perth whom he saved, who surely would have plummeted to her death in a day or two, unnoticed and undiscovered. I had never trained her to stay clear of deep wells.

In June, while the builders were sprucing the place up, we decided to squeeze in a holiday in the Scottish Highlands as a nostalgic return to the country that gave Perth her name. There was time for it before the birth of our baby. We drove up into the western Highlands and settled into a youth hostel on the River Dee amid the Grampian Mountains, a one-room stone cottage with a slate roof. A more deserted hostel cannot be imagined. We saw nobody. There was no electricity so we had to cook everything over an open fire, and at night we lit candles. There was no inside toilet either. The beds were thin mattresses up in a loft which we ascended by ladder. Since Perth insisted on sleeping with us, I had to carry her up the ladder. There we were, next to a rushing river of the purest water, surrounded by rocky and green mountains, with no human sounds to hear except our own. We meant to stay for one week, but the weather was fabulous and we stretched it to two.

Rising high in the Grampians, the River Dee flows swiftly

to the east in a succession of rapids, pools and arching bends through lush pastures and rich forests. Sheep were everywhere. The river by the hostel was shallow, rapid and freezing. But in the sunshine we persuaded ourselves to jump in. The water rushed down over the rocks and Perth swam strongly against the current. She climbed on to rocky ledges and positioned herself so the water could fall in a noisy torrent on her head and back. The three of us took long, lonely hikes in the forests and across the sides of mountains, through some of the wildest landscape of gorse and heather I had ever seen in Britain. But for entire days Perth was on her own. We never knew where she was, although once on our own climbs we did run into her near the top of one of the peaks. She smelled clean and pure. Her eyes were as clear as the sky. At night she lay motionless with fatigue, her eyes rolling and muscles twitching in sleep.

We all knew these days were precious, a last adventure together when it was just the three of us. Soon we would be four and Perth sensed it. At times she seemed to sulk, her ears held low and eyes looking hurt. She perked up when she was on the move, but around us she looked as if she was trying to understand what seemed different. It may have been our conversation, for we were full of talk about the baby with a tone and attitude that were unfamiliar to her. I think we talked less often to her and more often to each other. She felt a bit neglected, on the margin. Alert dogs who are spiritually tuned into their masters and mistresses can pick up the slightest hints of changes. For most of her life, Perth had been able to sense when I was troubled, afraid, unhappy or angry, even if I never said anything. At such times she could be as comforting as a wife or sister. Now, however, the change in the air was more basic and far-reaching, and she knew it.

135

Did she fear we were about to leave her again for months, worried she would land back in a kennel? Did it occur to her that she should run away when she had the chance? The Scottish Highlands were at her feet. She could be gone and never again have her life darkened by the threat of kennel walls and cages. She had had her fill of them. But how could she leave us, whom she loved? She was our soul-sister. With the sounds of the rushing waters filling the nights, she drew closer to us than usual.

Chapter 17

When Andrew was born in August, Perth at last knew what
had been worrying her. Everything was perfect for her at
Appletree Cottage until then. The sunny days, peaceful
village, comfortable garden, mysterious cottage and exquisite
landscape beckoning on the other side of the hedge were for
her absolute contentment. The three of us had moved in
quickly and settled into the most wonderful way of life any
of us had ever known, an idyll if ever there was one. While
Perth slipped away for a morning of running and searching,
Cindy and I had our routine, one that we would repeat year
after year: reading and writing in the morning, lunches of
cheeses and summer salads and fruits, afternoon walks on the
Downs or along the river, afternoon tea on the rolling
smooth-shaven lawn, a later dinner, more reading, and then
bed with the French door of our bedroom wide open letting
in the sounds, smells and dim twilight views of the countryside
all around us. Perth generally spent the mornings on the run,
but after lunch she stayed the rest of the day with us. The
rural and domestic stability of our lives was precious.

Then it ended for us all. The baby's arrival was not quiet.
He made his presence felt from the start and we were all
thrown off balance, especially Perth who regarded him at first
as an odd-looking intruder. And he did look a sight with
almost no hair and a round Mr Magoo face. For several weeks

he refused to sleep peaceably. Perth always slept with us in the room next to Andrew's so she got an unwelcome earful of his crying. Her escape from the baby's outbursts was to dive into dark, muffled safety under our covers. There she would wait until the emergency was over. After a few weeks she took these interruptions more in her stride, but she disliked our getting in and out of bed so many times. So did we but all we could do was wait and hope that Andrew would soon find his own peaceful rhythms and join the three of us in ours.

During the day everything was similarly turned upside down. Hardly anything except our meals happened in the way and at the time they used to. There was a lot of scurrying around, seeing to this and that emergency, getting something for the baby, cleaning and feeding the baby, walking the baby, holding the baby. Just when we had settled down in the garden to relax with a book and a pot of tea, Andrew would cry out that he needed something.

Perth had never known anything like it in our family. In the mornings she escaped for hours through the hedge. She usually made for the river first. Down there in late summer and early autumn the lush green banks teemed with ducks, geese, swans, many kinds of rodents and rabbits to keep her interest. She worked her way several miles up and down the river, sniffing into thousands of mysterious holes. At the deep bottom of many of them busy little 'households' of wildlife as in *The Wind in the Willows* carried on without being in the least disturbed by her. But she could smell the warm, furry beasts down there, and she passed from hole to hole hoping some day to see where these enticing odours were coming from. Then she would launch herself into the fields, now just stubble after the harvests, and make her way into the hills. At times she did not return until late afternoon, sometimes not until the evening, dirty, panting and thirsty.

In those early weeks after Andrew's arrival, there was one thing in particular that worried us. When we put him on the soft grass to lie, or on the carpet in the living room, and Perth was there, too, how would she treat him? We knew she would never lick him. She would sniff, certainly. But babies wave their arms and legs suddenly, and they crawl about. What if Perth were in a deep sleep on the grass and Andrew silently crept up to her and, as a baby might, placed his head heavily and roughly on hers? Would she just get up and walk away, or would she do what she had done to other nuisance heads in her lifetime? Snap at it.

I spoke to her about this. Lying on the grass beside her, I put my own head next to hers as she lay there, and pleaded with her to understand that Andrew was tiny and helpless, that when he got older he would be a great friend and companion to her. She needed to be patient. Things would get better.

'Whatever you do, dogge,' I whispered into her ear, 'don't you snap at him, especially at his face. If you did, it might leave a mark on his face for the rest of his life. I know it'll be hard if he crawls all over you and mauls you with his arms. But just move away and leave him be. Please, Perth, don't get angry and impatient at him. Think of me and your mistress.' She was as beautiful as ever, lying there on the grass. And strong. We could only hope that the trust she knew we had in her would be enough to protect Andrew. One thing we knew: we would never separate them. They must learn to live together. On the bed or lawn we would often lie with Perth between Andrew and us, hugging them both, so that she never felt neglected.

Andrew did maul her many times, and when we saw it happening our hearts missed a beat or two. Most of the time she simply ignored him. She had grudgingly accepted the encroacher, but that was about all.

Three or four weeks after Andrew's birth we did something that changed Perth's behaviour towards him. With Andrew in a backpack strapped on my shoulders, we all climbed up to the Downs. We wanted to let the landscape into his imagination as early as possible. Perhaps as a result he would in some mystical way bond with nature. He would become one of its disciples, free-spirited and bold. Now, many will think this is balderdash, the vain thoughts of proud parents with delusions of grandeur for their child. Others will feel that this was far too early and risky to take an infant up to the windy hills for a hike of several miles. But Andrew loved it, never crying once. Uncharacteristically, Perth stayed with us the whole time. Something happened along the way to change her feelings about the baby. I think it was that Andrew now was in her world. She saw him staring out over the landscape a thousand feet below, his face pink from the cool wind, eyes wide open. She saw him differently, no longer part of the claustrophobic baby world that Appletree Cottage had become for her. He had been liberated. It is worth mentioning that when Andrew grew up you could not keep him off the Downs. He walked the eighty-mile length of them several times. And as soon as he was old enough, he and Perth spent many hours wandering up there together in isolated exploration, year after year.

From that day on, she loved him. It was to her as if he had become someone real. She stayed with him in the garden, allowed him to climb on her, and played with him. When we carried him down to the river for walks, she lay down next to his carry-cot by the sparkling water and watched over him while Cindy and I strolled along the river. Often she climbed into armchairs with him and slept by his side. If we were on the sofa together, she jumped up and took her place between us and him. She never bit him.

Having made this adjustment so completely and quickly, she had no trouble welcoming Andrew's sister, Claire, when she was born three years later. In fact, it was while Cindy was having Claire in the maternity hospital in Rustington nearby on the Sussex coast that Perth made another hospital visit. I had just left Cindy and was walking on the pebbly beach with Perth before returning home. I took no notice when Perth turned back to the hospital. Apparently she walked through the front door, turned left into the correct corridor, her nails clicking on the floor rhythmically as she trotted along, and effortlessly found Cindy's room. Cindy was nursing Claire, so Perth hopped on her bed. With her previous hospital experience, Cindy took it in her stride. The nurses this time were not at all happy when they saw Perth, but it was all as it should have been.

Claire took to Perth as naturally as Andrew did. Before she was able to walk, she could often be found in Perth's basket in the kitchen, sharing the space with her. So that often she took on that intoxicating groggy-doggie smell. As soon as she could walk, she took to climbing on Perth's back for rides in the garden, Perth heaving under her weight uncomplainingly. Tired of those antics, they would then lie down together on the grass beneath our ancient apple tree on an old blanket that I still had from my boyhood at St George's College in Argentina. Claire had joined the club.

Chapter 18

I do wonder if Perth ever thought back much to those dislocating years in America and the bitter months in quarantine, whether images ever flashed upon her inward eye of her innocence in Cazenovia, crashing into Frederick the St Bernard, getting mistreated by me at Agnes Roy Camp and running lost and alone in Vermont, being chained up in a dark barn like a common criminal, scrambling through the thickets beside the ocean surf in Florida, grubbily anointing herself with the garbage in Ohio, or being heartbroken that we were leaving her yet again in the summer for another trip to England. It is enough for the reader to know that the years in Appletree Cottage with our growing family passed with a certainty and regularity that she never had across the ocean.

She grew older, into her teens, without the pains of separation from her family that she had known in America. As the years wore on, her love for Andrew and Claire deepened, and her relationship with them changed as they changed. We were all part of a team, ever changing, and Perth was at the centre of it. For Cindy and me she was the living link between our early married life in America without children and our English incarnation in Appletree Cottage with family and far richer lives. For years Perth watched Cindy get on the train regularly for London to study for her postgraduate degree. And she witnessed the excitement as I published a couple of books. In fact, she helped me write them. I spent many hours talking to her about my ideas as she listened alertly, not interrupting, giving me a sense of comfort that whatever readers might think about my writing she at least was behind me. When once I read an unkind review of one of my books in the newspaper, it was she in whom I confided my despair and who restored my spirits. She was just there.

That was the way it had always been with her, but she had moved into a phase of her life in which she was not only an astounding runner and tireless adventurer in the open air, a disciplined spirit who would not suffer fools gladly, but also a quieter and gentler sympathiser. We all relied on her. Even the village had come to accept her as a colourful local figure. She had become something of a village legend.

The old Perth, however, still thrived. She often flirted with danger, almost as if she were testing her own invincibility. On a high coastal walk one October along the cliffs of Dorset, for example, when she was fourteen, she could have been blown to bits. The British Army for years had tested land mines in large fields overlooking the sea. The fields were fenced off and loaded with mines. The five of us were walking merrily along on this October morning, enjoying the scenery of sea and cliffs, when suddenly to the right we noticed a sign that read, 'EXTREME CAUTION: LAND MINES. BRITISH ARMY.' At precisely that moment Perth decided to veer off the path. She made for the fence, found a hole in it, and in no time at all was walking among the mines. The field was lush, deceptive. Lurking underneath its inviting greenness was death. For Perth it was fun; for us it was intense panic. Helpless, we stared at her. Claire was only three and had no idea of any danger. Andrew, however, knew better. He went white.

How could I warn her? If I yelled at her and madly waved my arms, I might provoke her to run all over the place, to her certain destruction. Calmly, I shouted very firmly, 'Stay, Perth, stay!' I repeated it. She froze and looked back at us, about one hundred feet away. 'Good dog, now stay.' She did not move.

My training sessions with her on East Lake Road in Cazenovia came back to me. Would she obey me now? I then shouted to her with great severity, so that she was under no illusion that we were playing games, 'Come HERE, dogge, HERE, HERE!' I had to persuade her to come straight back to us. If she kept to a straight line, there was less chance she would walk on a mine. I held my hand up with my finger pointed down to the ground in front of me. 'HERE,' I repeated. I glared at her. Andrew placed his hands over his eyes. She turned and walked slowly back, safely through the hole in the fence. None of us said anything. We took deep breaths and walked on.

I think it was that same year, in late November in East Sussex, that she almost met her Maker on another stretch of coastline, Beachy Head. We had never been there before, though my father used to speak fondly of it to me when I was a boy in America. It is an open stretch of Downland, windswept and wild, several hundred feet above some sheer cliffs that fall vertically right down to the sea. A treacherous stretch of coastline with unpredictable currents, over the centuries sailors have been blown ashore there and perished on the rocks. The springy turf of the Downs sweeps above, a great place for running at full throttle.

We knew nothing of the configurations of this landscape until we got there, and then it was almost too late. The five of us set off marching across the open turf towards the sea.

144

When we got close enough, I could see that there was no fence or barrier to mark where the earth stopped and the void beyond began. Nothing to warn the unsuspecting. I thought of the blind and suicidal Gloucester in Shakespeare's terrible tragedy *King Lear*, in legendary medieval England, who asks his son to lead him across the wasteland to the edge of a steep cliff above the crashing sea. Once there he plans to fall to his certain destruction. His son leads him instead to a harmless bit of land where he falls over without injury. Then I caught sight of Perth racing recklessly for the edge, totally unaware that in a few metres she was bound to launch herself into the abyss. Another, more tragic, literary incident suddenly made me shudder, the one from Thomas Hardy's *Far from the Madding Crowd* in which Gabriel Oak's sheepdog, possessed by some primeval urge, herds every one of his flock straight off a Dorset cliff and on to the rocks a couple of hundred feet below.

At the speed Perth was nearing the edge I was sure she was doomed. Nonetheless, I sprinted towards the sea, yelling to her to stop, to stay, to come back. With the wind gusting she could not hear. There was nothing I could do but watch helplessly. Perhaps she had her own primeval instincts, though, because with only a few feet to go, she dug her nails in the turf and pushed with all her strength to veer off to the right. She came to a stop with her body stretched along the edge. When I ran up, she was still there, panting, looking down at the foaming sea below where the majestic lighthouse flashed its lights in warning to the reckless.

Occasionally, it was her turn to panic. Early one July morning at about seven o'clock, Andrew and I decided to take a pre-breakfast walk to the meadow, on the way down to the river. He was four. Perth came with us. We did this often together during that summer. It was a lovely still morning with a heavy dew on the grass. We walked through the 'kissing gate' into the meadow, shutting it carefully behind us with that characteristic click of the latch. There spread out near the gate in front of us, lazily munching on the wet grass, were ten or so of Barbara Stapeley's lovely brown Guernsey cows. Barbara owned a small dairy farm at the bottom of Bury Hollow, a stone's throw down the hill from Appletree Cottage. Andrew loved her cows because of their kind-looking eyes. We stopped to rub some of their heads. As we were walking by, I noticed that one of my shoelaces was loose, so I stopped and leaned down to tie it. I made too tempting a target for one of the cows, I guess, who while I was bent over jumped at the opportunity to mount me from behind. I could not imagine what she had in mind. Raising herself on her hind legs, she landed on my back. Under her weight I fell heavily to the ground underneath her. Andrew saw it all and screamed. He thought he had lost his dad. Perth flew at the cow, howling ferociously. It was one of those times when she only made matters worse, for she terrified the cow and all her friends into a stampede. Mercifully, the hoofs of the overly friendly one on top of me barely missed my head as she leapt away. I struggled to my feet, unhurt.

Chapter 19

Except for frequent incidents like these, the years passed peacefully and Perth grew to a great age. She never became fat, nor did she stop scouting the countryside, but she did slow down. Her muscles got a bit smaller. Her coat still shone, but her blackness turned greyish and the brown along her muzzle became flecked with white. At sixteen, her eyes were as good as ever, although her hearing very gradually declined. She may have been old, but she was nobody's fool. People knew well enough not to take liberties with her, especially not to try to pick her up or, as always, put their heads down to hers. Appletree Cottage had been the scene of four or five awkward moments when guests had been on the receiving end of a fast tooth of hers. Many more had been snapped at and escaped without a wound. Barbara Stapeley, one of Perth's more understanding friends, called her 'Fang'. A bit ridiculous, one might think, since Perth was then the venerable age of sixteen. But perhaps not?

It was that year that I was offered a Visiting Associate Professorship at the College of William and Mary in Virginia for nine months. It sounded stimulating. Claire had not yet set foot in America. Andrew had been to Florida once to see his grandmother, but only as a toddler. On top of that, Cindy and I wanted to get back to the States for a few months. It was nine years since we had left it. But what would we do with Perth? Here we were again, trying to figure out the eternal problem.

A kennel was out. We looked around for friends without children whom we thought might like to have a beagle for nine months. It was too risky to place Perth in a house with children who did not know how to behave with her. One midsummer evening at dinner as Cindy and I turned the problem over in our minds, I had an idea.

'What about Alistair and Stella Shaw on Church Lane? They're young and sensible, with no kids or complications of that sort. They might like to have Perth around for a few months. I saw him stroking her the other day.'

'That's brilliant,' Cindy replied. 'She teaches at the local school, so she gets home early every day. Perth could even visit her at the school. It's only across the lane from where they live.'

'What does Alistair do?'

'He works in a local vineyard near Arundel.'

'Perfect. Perth could keep them company there, too. She'd love running in and out of the grapevines.'

Alistair Shaw, a handsome and slender young man in his mid-twenties who sported a generous and stylish moustache, was a chef at the weekends, but at the vineyard his job was to keep the vines trimmed and properly tied to the wooden supports. The vineyard, nestled in some gentle vales half way up the southern slopes of the Downs, was well known for its white wine. Alistair and Stella were a simple, hard-working couple. Their house was one of those tiny semi-detached dwellings built between the wars, with a functional garden in the back just large enough for a table, chairs and some vegetables. I had always liked them.

We walked down to see them the next day. We put the idea

to them and were amazed when they jumped at it.

'Oh, we'd love to have Perth,' Stella piped up. 'Perth is so sweet. We've so much wanted a dog. How old is she?' All eyes turned to Perth for a moment in silence. She was sitting on the carpet looking at me, her ears perked up and alert. She understood what was going on, but seemed untroubled.

'Believe it or not, she's sixteen,' I answered.

'Really!' said Alistair. 'She's in great shape. I see her running around all over the place. She could come with me to the vineyard, as long as she doesn't eat the grapes off the vines!' He laughed.

That remark made me a little uncomfortable. I thought of the strawberries in the Huntington Gardens in California and of a journey years ago that Cindy, Perth and I made by car from Boston to St Andrews in New Brunswick, Canada, when Perth was five. Somewhere in Canada on a lonely road our Rover broke down, and while we were trying to coax it to start Perth had quietly rummaged around in the bushes on the roadside. She had discovered some blueberry bushes and was methodically and gingerly picking the succulent berries off them. She must have eaten dozens by the time we noticed her. Her mouth was stained blue and her breath smelled wonderfully fruity. She looked quite pleased with herself. It was not a great leap of the imagination to see her devouring a large portion of Alistair's crop of white Sussex grapes. But I said nothing.

'You can let her run loose,' I said. 'You don't have to bother walking her anywhere.'

The Shaws were so enthusiastic that it was agreed on the spot we would have a trial run. Beginning the next day they would take Perth for a week, and if they still wanted her after that, so be it. I told them I'd bring down the basket in which she slept, along with a few tins of food. There was nothing else she needed. Before leaving, I stressed one thing.

'You've got to remember one very important thing. You'll love Perth. She's an amazing dog. But don't try to take food away from her, or come up to her from behind and attempt to pick her up. She doesn't like to be picked up, especially by surprise. Remember, her hearing is not what it used to be. Most important of all, don't put your head down to hers. She doesn't like it, okay?'

So, the next morning I brought her down with her basket and food, had a cup of coffee with the Shaws, and hoped that we had indeed found a good solution this time. It was a perfect arrangement: Perth could stay in Bury and still be able to come and go as she pleased. The Shaws were quiet and steady, liked dogs and had no children. It was a good sign that after I told her to 'stay,' Perth did not try to follow me when I left.

The following day was Sunday. After church we devoured one of Cindy's roast lambs for lunch and were taking up our positions in the garden to read when the phone rang. It was an unknown woman's voice, frantic.

'Will you come down immediately to get your dog. There's been an accident.' She hung up.

'Oh no, I think something's happened to Perth,' I cried, running into the garden. Cindy looked horror-struck. Andrew and Claire shouted for more information.

'Some woman told me there's been an accident. That's all I know. I'm going right down.' I sprinted across the meadow and down to the Shaw's house. In three minutes I was there. Pausing at the front gate to catch my breath, I could hear nothing. Nobody seemed to be at home. I lifted the latch and opened the gate. The front door was wide open. As I approached it, Perth walked out.

'Perth, you're all right! Thank God!' I shouted as I took her in my arms. 'Somebody said there was an accident. I thought you'd drowned in the river or something. Where are the Shaws?'

She was strangely passive. I walked up to the door which led directly into the kitchen. When I stepped in, the sight shocked me. I could scarcely believe what I saw. There was blood everywhere. There was blood on the floor next to her food bowl, and a trickle of it lead to the basin, which was spattered with it. The phone book was open and also stained with it, as if someone panicking had leafed through it to find a number. It was open to the yellow pages with the numbers of doctors.

I had no trouble piecing together what had happened. The 'accident' had occurred by Perth's food bowl. She must have been eating when someone came up to her from behind and tried to grab hold of her. Probably not hearing the person approach, she had swung around and sank her teeth into something. From the amount of blood and the stained phone book and telephone, it looked to me that she had found a hand or wrist. But whose hand? And how badly was it wounded?

Moaning to myself and imagining the worst, I staggered outside. There was Perth, waiting, the picture of guilt. She lowered her head. Her tail was between her legs.

'Perth, how can you do this?' I was almost crying. 'You've gone too far this time, you wicked dog. This may be the end of you. You've spoiled everything.' I walked out and she followed behind meekly with her tail between her legs.

At home the scene was dismal. Cindy was desperate with

worry over who had been hurt and how badly. Andrew and Claire were talking to Perth on the sunny grass. The contrast of that scene with what I had just seen on Church Lane was stark. We had trouble getting information but finally tracked the Shaws down by phone at St Richard's Hospital in the old Roman town of Chichester. I assured the nurse that Perth had had all the vaccinations she was supposed to have.

Perth had sunk her teeth into Alistair's right hand. He was having stitches and would not be home until the evening. Having imagined something much worse – I do not know what – we were momentarily relieved. But it was bad enough. In the evening, I rang up the Shaws and talked to Stella, who understandably sounded cold and unfriendly. I went straight down. They had cleaned up the kitchen and were both sitting by the table. Alistair's hand was heavily bandaged. I sat down with them and we talked.

'Well,' Alistair began, 'I guess it was my fault because I did just what you told me not to do. You warned me. I tried to pick her up. But that dog of yours is something else. You know, I don't think you should ever leave her with a friend. An enemy, perhaps. Anyway, I'll be all right. It doesn't hurt.'

'I'm so sorry, Alistair, and you too, Stella. Cindy is in anguish over this. It was all my fault because I wanted so much to find a nice place for her. It'll be so long, you see, that we'll be gone. I should have known better. Please forgive me.' I was still trembling.

We kept talking and eventually calmed down. I rang Cindy to tell her how things were.

'The problem is,' said Stella, 'Alistair now can't work at the vineyard for about three weeks. Our unemployment insurance covers only sixty per cent of his wages there. He can still be a chef, but that's only at weekends.'

I was hard at work on a project that summer and every minute was precious, but I did not hesitate.

'Don't worry. I'll work for you, Alistair.'

They stared at me. 'How could you?' Stella asked sceptically. 'You have to be trained in the vineyard.' I think she thought I was just trying to make myself feel better by offering, when in fact I was perfectly serious. How could we let the weeks roll by knowing that they were out of pocket because of Perth?

'Can't you train me, Alistair, just enough to help you keep on top of things there? Let's drive over tomorrow and you can explain everything to me.'

'Well, that's very decent of you. I won't pretend it won't really be helpful to us. Can you spare the time?'

'Yes, of course. If I do okay, I can stick with it until you can start back.'

We settled on it. As I walked home, I wondered if I hadn't been too impetuous in offering. This would play havoc with my own work. I'd have to work late into the nights for a long stretch to make up for time lost. But it had to be. Cindy thought I had done the right thing.

'As for you,' I said to Perth firmly when I got home, 'you're going with me to the vineyard. I don't see why I have to be there on my own all day while you're having a great time here.' She knew I was extremely angry with her. There was no point in trying to punish her physically, though. She was penitent enough and at her age there was nothing any of us could do to make her mend her ways. Part of her strength was part of her liability. We could only hope that this sort of thing would never happen again. It was lucky it was not worse.

Alistair taught me the mysteries of viniculture and I ended

up working at the vineyard for three solid weeks. It was tedious work. Most of what I did every day was 'tuck' the vines behind wiring, up and down monotonous rows of plants. One benefit, I suppose, was that it got me out of my study and into the fresh Sussex air. Perth came with me every day and I forced her to sit around and do nothing hour after hour. It was the worst kind of punishment for her. At the end of the three weeks Alistair's hand had healed well enough to allow him to return to work. He was very grateful. In three months his hand was perfectly restored. There was no sign of Perth's attack except the stitch marks which were fast disappearing. Stella remained cool and distant. She never resumed her friendship with us. Neither of them ever wanted to see Perth again.

Chapter 20

After that debacle we were no nearer to finding Perth a place for nine months. We would be gone in late August and time was wearing thin. A private family was now out of the question. There was nothing left but to find a kennel. But this time we were lucky. Before our feet life's pearls were cast. The logical choice was Barbara Stapeley who in addition to keeping beautiful and rumbustious cows ran a small business on her farm called Bury Hollow Kennels, only two hundred metres down from the bottom of our garden.

Barbara Stapeley was one of those unforgettable characters such as you read about in popular human interest magazines. She was in her seventies and very robust. A large round woman with a florid, circular face, she had short grey hair that was always tousled, as if she had just emerged from a violent windstorm. I do not remember ever having seen her in any fine clothing. She wore plain shirts and dungarees, jeans, or denim overalls wherever she went. For decades in Bury she had bred smooth fox terriers and curly-coated retrievers for which she was famous throughout the world, winning prize after prize for them at the prestigious annual Crufts Dog Show in London. She was no-nonsense and plain-speaking, highly educated and extremely intelligent.

People were always surprised by how brusque she could be. The people in the company that for fifty years picked up her milk to transport it to the dairy decided one day that her driveway was too narrow for their lorries. The lorries had not widened, neither had her driveway narrowed, but for some reason they felt they needed more room. She refused to do anything to her driveway. They informed her then that they could no longer collect her milk. With a wave of her hand she said, fine, sold her cows, and went out of the dairy business permanently. Rather than bicker with fussy administrators whose arrogant ideas of modern methods and conveniences she found irritating and a threat to old rural ways and values, she said to heck with them and concentrated on her kennel. She kept a few of the cows dearest to her for old times' sake.

Late one November night one of those cows got through her fence into the sloping meadow between her cottage and ours. Awakened by her dogs, Barbara followed the beast by moonlight and found that it had worked its way through some other fencing at the upper part of the meadow. It was paralysed with fear between the fence and the edge of the greensand stone cliff, thirty feet above the Hollow. Barbara could not budge it, so at about midnight she knocked or rather beat upon our back door for my help. I came out with Perth who did her bit by howling at the cow to get her to move. The three of us struggled for an hour, under the cold November moonlight, before we were able to coax the cow back to safety. Barbara was like that. She never stood on ceremony or wasted time with decorum.

Many people were offended by her brusqueness and candour. We loved her big, compassionate heart. And she understood dogs better than anyone I have ever known. She had fathomed the mysteries and eccentricities of Perth from the moment we moved into the village. What she recognised in her was an indomitable will and a keen intelligence, a restless animal with a triple portion of pluck. She could see that Perth had to be given unlimited space, and she had little patience with anyone who suggested that the dog should be tied up. But she also detected a streak of nervousness, a fierce impatience, that she thought could be traced to the number of times we had abandoned Perth for travel over the years.

'If Perth were average, a regular and docile pet,' she once said to us, 'you wouldn't have had any trouble. But the way you've brought her up to believe that she is entitled to perfect freedom has made her not only a survivor but also hard to control. She also trusts you profoundly. That's another problem. I think she thinks you let her down sometimes.'

Now Perth was sixteen and we had to leave her behind again. It was out of the question for her to come with us, not unless we were willing to put her into quarantine for six more cruel months when we returned. At her age, that would kill her. We were all deeply dejected not only over the whole idea of abandoning her, but also over the prospect of being without her for so long.

In the early part of what was a cold August, shortly before the wheat and barley were harvested and with only two weeks to go before we were to be wrenched away, something both comic and pathetic occurred that made it still clearer to us we could never leave Perth with a family, however well meaning and capable the family might be. Apart from her hearing and greyness, it was a sign that she was getting older. Barbara Stapeley played the comic part in this, Perth the pathetic part.

Again, in the dead of night, we were awakened by the telephone ringing. It was Barbara.

'For heaven's sake, don't you hear Perth out in the wheat

howling? She's lost in it. Grab your torch and get out there and find her. The poor animal.'

'Barbara,' I replied croakily and disbelievingly, 'if there's one thing Perth could never be it's lost in the wheat. She must have cornered a vole or something. It'll be over in a minute. Let's go back to sleep.' I could now hear Perth. She certainly was raising a din.

'Peter, you grab your torch and get out there,' she said impatiently. 'I know that beagle of yours and I can tell a frenzied howl when I hear it. If you're too lazy to rouse yourself, ask your better half to explore. Can't you hear Perth? She's frantic.'

'I don't think we have a torch,' I answered, truthfully.

'Then come down here and borrow mine!' She hung up.

When Barbara commanded, one obeyed. So Cindy threw on her clothes and hurried down the pitch darkness of the Hollow to the kennels, walked around the back and knocked on Barbara's kitchen door. She answered immediately. She was wrapped up in a large, tattered fur coat.

'Well, what took you so long? Hurry, here's the torch. Go on, go on. This cold will be the end of me. I've got absolutely nothing on under this coat. And when you find her, pick her up and carry her across the wheat. There's something the matter with her.'

Without looking too carefully at Barbara in her coat, Cindy hurried back up the Hollow. I was dressed by then and together through a gap in the hedge we stepped out into the field. Perth was still howling. Immediately we almost stumbled on a rare sight. There in front of us the wheat had been levelled down in a small circle, in the centre of which lay a family of hedgehogs – mother, father and four babies. They were all looking up at our bright torch, their beady eyes wide open, gleaming in the light. We had momentarily disturbed their cosy nest.

'How sweet!' Cindy whispered. 'Careful, don't disturb them.' We moved on into the dark, walking through the tall wheat along a tractor track in the direction of the noise. Perth was not hard to find. In about five minutes we came upon her. She was just standing there, surrounded by the wheat, thoroughly disoriented, howling. She had no idea which direction was the way home. Something had failed her. She stopped the noise when she saw us and melted in our arms. I gathered her up and with Cindy leading with the torch we made our way back to the garden. When I put her down on the grass, she was perfectly all right. The three of us got back into bed quickly and Perth took up her usual position between the sheets. The children were still asleep, having heard none of the commotion.

Nothing like this had ever happened to Perth. Her nose, eyes and ears had failed her. Was it a sign of things to come? Could we no longer rely on her sense of direction? What if this happened to her one day three miles from home? Barbara had heard the sounds and known what they meant.

I also knew that Barbara liked a half-pint of cider at the Black Dog and Duck across the lane around lunchtime, so Perth and I tracked her down there the next day. She was sitting in the small saloon 'Juscumin' bar with a friend.

'Barbara, I've been looking for you. May I join you for a minute or two?'

'Of course. Hello, Perth, are we all right now?' She was in a good mood, I could tell. Perth sat down next to her feet.

'After that incident last night, I need to talk to you about Perth. We're in a fix. You know, we're leaving for America in a couple of weeks.'

'Yes, I know, I know. And you want me to take Perth.'

'Perth is a remarkable dog, you know, Barbara.'

'She has to be a remarkable dog to have a master like you.' Her friend got a chuckle out of that.

'We were hoping to leave her with a family, but that fiasco with the Shaws killed that idea.' I scratched Perth's head.

'Peter, you should've asked me sooner. You were insane to think you could leave a dog of that age with a young couple who know nothing about dogs, especially one with a mind of her own like Perth. Of course I'll take her, though I've never before taken a dog for that length of time. I'll do it for Perth.'

'I could kiss you!' I blurted out recklessly.

'If you do, the deal is off,' she shot back with a smile. 'You realise she'll stay in the 'dormitory' in the kennel, not in the house?'

'Yes.'

'But I'll take good care of her. She'll go on walks, I'll bring in a strong heat lamp and she'll get the best food. I'll bring her into the house, too, from time to time. And you can pay me the going quarantine rates.'

'Perfect.' Perth was listening to this, undoubtedly understanding the arrangement, apparently untroubled.

'Well, old girl,' Barbara said to her as she stroked her head, 'what do you think about that? You'll be all right with me, don't you worry'. Looking at me, she added, 'I know you like Perth to run loose, but I can't accept the responsibility of allowing that. You'd never forgive me if she fell down a well or was hit by a car.'

'I know. It's a rotten thing we're doing leaving her.' In my guilt, I had to justify myself. 'But, Barbara, I can't pass up this opportunity in the States.'

Shades of past summer agonies darkened my mind as I

spoke to her. I was actually going down this path again, only in reverse. I could not bring myself to tell her of my former peregrinations during Perth's early years in America.

'Fine, fine, come down and we'll work out the details. I know you and Cindy love Perth. I can tell it runs deep.'

The next few days passed quickly. On our last day in England we took Perth down to Barbara.

'Don't worry about her,' Barbara said cheerfully. She could see we were in a bad way. 'I'll keep her warm and she'll be among friends. Right, old girl? Write to me from time to time and I'll write back and let you know how she's doing. She looks perfectly fit so she'll do fine.'

'Thanks, Barbara,' Cindy replied, her eyes moist. 'She's our first child, you know.'

'Come on, I'll show you right now where she'll be living.' She took us into the 'dormitory', what used to be a barn for the hay. It was dry and sweet-smelling. There was only one other, very quiet, dog in there. Perth's run was large. Its floor was covered with fresh straw and there was a spacious dog house inside it for her to curl up in. From an adjacent barn we could hear the sounds of hens and geese. Close by in the fields were horses and cows. It could not have been better. She was safe, loved and comfortable in a farmyard setting, so unlike that agrarian Hades in Vermont from which she had fled so many years before. The only thing she lacked was perfect liberty to come and go.

Chapter 21

It is useless to complain of all those months we spent in Virginia without Perth. Life was crammed with new experiences and the nine months flew by. Andrew and Claire grew up a good deal that year. They never forgot Perth but America was full of excitement for them, especially at Colonial Williamsburg, the eighteenth-century outdoor museum where they saw early American history brought to life in hundreds of intriguing ways. Pottery, shoes and boots, candles, garden tools, musical instruments and much more were all made before their eyes in architecturally authentic wooden-frame houses and shops. For two children who had grown up in a cottage built just about the time Christopher Columbus was discovering 'America', these buildings did not seem that antique, but they were charmed by people dressed up in eighteenth-century clothing and the feeling of being lifted out of the twentieth century. It was like walking into a storybook.

It was for me, too. The College of William and Mary is a venerable institution, the second oldest university in America. The Wren Building, where I taught, is the oldest academic building in the country. My office, a separate 'kitchen' dating from the late seventeenth-century, is the most ancient existing academic office in North America. I got a bit fed up with tourists who kept coming by, peeking in and asking me how old the building was, whether George Washington had ever walked in it, whether Thomas Jefferson had slept there. But it was all fun. I played on the faculty tennis team, gave lectures to schools throughout Tidewater, Virginia and even ran in several thirteen-mile half-marathons. The American lifestyle still did not suit me, I discovered after ten years' absence, but there were compensations.

Still, we pined for Perth. While all this was going on, three thousand miles away she stayed healthy and according to Barbara seemed even to enjoy her time at Hollow Farm Kennels. Barbara saw to it that she had plenty to eat and plenty of exercise. She was an artist with Perth, perfectly in tune with her moods and temperament. Perth loved her. They were in many ways very similar, two older ladies with strong ideas about how life should be lived, in no doubt about whom they liked and disliked and not the slightest bit reluctant to tell them so. Perth was single-minded, even there. Early on, she claimed the fifth or end run in the 'dormitory' as her own. If Barbara ever happened to put a visiting dog in the fifth run while Perth was out in the yard, on her return Perth would stubbornly and quietly take up a position in front of that run and refuse to budge until the interloper was evicted. Make no mistake about it, Barbara had fallen in love with Perth.

When we boarded the plane in May to return to England, my mind jerked back guiltily to those painful times many years earlier when leaving America meant abandoning Perth for months. But flying out of America now meant a joyful return to her after our longest separation in her long life. In a few hours we would be reunited with her in Appletree Cottage and she would be at large again, reborn in the cradle of greenness of our adopted country. She was now seventeen but surely she could pick up where she left off. Or could she?

163

What would she be like after ten months of being pent up? Would she be her old self or had these months turned her into an old dog?

We drove into Bury and made straight for the kennel. Barbara greeted the four of us in her dressing gown. She looked a sight. We were a little taken back as we had become used to everyone in Williamsburg always dressing so neatly and crisply. There was none of Bury's rural roughness there. She was unsentimental in welcoming us back but delighted for Perth's sake. There were no massive hugs, just light kisses on the cheeks.

'This is a golden day for your lovely beagle,' she said. 'You're not going to leave again next week, are you, or next month? I'll strike you off my list of desirables if you do. She's been wonderful, a real trooper. A bit stiffer in the joints, but some good running will put that right. Hang on, and I'll get her.'

Perth stuck her nose out of the barn door and trotted out. Andrew saw her first and rushed to her, meeting her halfway across the yard in a blur of joy. The rest of us followed. I had never seen her looking better. Her coat was shiny, her chest white, her body slim. She howled constantly. Barbara watched it all amused and immensely satisfied.

'Barbara, she looks fantastic,' I shouted in the middle of it all. 'I can't thank you enough for caring for her – but what's more important, for loving her. She'll live a long time still.' Andrew and Claire both stepped up to Barbara and shook her hand.

'Thank you, Miss Stapeley, for making Perth look so good,' Andrew said.

When we walked into the garden of Appletree Cottage, my emotions came rushing on. Back at last! Everything was so beautiful. This was our only home. It took no time at all for us all to pick up our lives in Bury, and Perth promptly launched herself into the green world. It was late spring, the new roses were blooming, lambs and calves were luxuriating in the freshness of the season, and there was so much for her to see and do. She stretched her legs and called upon long-unused muscles to propel her once again through the acres of fragrant Sussex earth.

Barbara was right, however. She did seem stiffer and she moved more slowly. She was still gone most mornings, but she covered less ground. Her spirit was as willing as ever, but her body was weaker. It seemed to me impossible, though, a contradiction of the elements that made up her being, that she could ever quit or stop. She would probably be running until the moment she stopped breathing. In human years, she was already the equivalent of 119, like one of those Old Testament matriarchs who at enormous ages still walked through the deserts of the Middle East looking for the Promised Land. Perth long ago had found her Promised Land and was still investing it with new meaning. She knew every building, hedge, path, lane, hill, farm and garden in it. It seemed a world without end.

Winter came on early that year. It reminded us of Perth's last months in quarantine. In November there were already hard frosts, as well as dustings of snow. At eighteen Perth felt it severely. She began to hobble over the frozen grass. Barbara told us it was arthritis. For the first time she had difficulty climbing up and down the four steps from the kitchen out to the garden. Nor could she jump up on our bed any more. We took to lifting her up whenever she needed it. The alarming thing was that at odd moments she also began to twitch from her shoulders up. She looked as if she were having minor epileptic fits. 'Come and get Perth,' Jenny Dover called one day from across the lane, 'she's having one of her fits in my garden.'

Everything seemed to come upon her at once. Her eyesight began to fail. And at night she started being incontinent. We closed her in the kitchen with her basket so she could not foul up the carpets. She tried hard to control herself. If one of us was able to wake up by five in the morning to let her out, she was fine. But if we delayed until seven or so, we would come down to a puddle on the kitchen floor and often also a bowel movement. As the months passed, this became more regular. She would lie in her basket and look up at us apologetically as we opened the kitchen door in the morning and discovered the mess. We simply cleaned it up and there would be no more trouble until the next morning.

One day Andrew overheard me say in an unguarded moment, 'You know, Cindy, if this continues, will we be able to keep her?' It was at breakfast and I had just cleaned up a particularly messy floor as Perth slumbered in her basket.

Cindy put her hand on mine and said simply and quietly, 'You know perfectly well we would do anything for Perth as long as we need to. We might as well cut off our hands or legs as part with her.' I put my hand on hers. We looked at this remarkable dog in her basket, both overwhelmed with emotion. If only she could live for ever.

Early next morning when I descended groggily to the kitchen to deal with the usual mess, there was a little note on the table from Andrew. It read: 'Dear Mum and Dad. I'll clean up Perth's mess every morning. Don't worry. Please don't take her away. Love, Andrew.'

'My dear son, I love you so much,' I said to him later that day. 'Perth loves you, too. You're a dear heart to want to clean up after her. Let's take turns, how about that? It'll be like putting the kettle on in the morning. We won't think anything of it, we'll just do it. We'll never take her away, for any reason. She'll always be here with us.' A few days later Claire wrote a similar note.

For months after that, he dragged himself out of bed at five and cleaned up the floor, on his hands and knees with rags and a bucket of water. It was smelly and unpleasant work, but he was faithful and never missed his turn. Several mornings I found Claire on her hands and knees with him, scrubbing away silently.

Perth's hearing also got very bad, which made one of her last acts of heroism, if we can call it that, all the more amazing. One day Cindy and I were in our bedroom upstairs, idly chatting. Perth was on the bed with us. Suddenly, her head shot up; she looked towards the French door that overlooked the garden and fields. We had heard nothing, but she erupted into barks and howls, jumping off the bed and running to the window. Never mind her failing eyesight and hearing. There was something out there.

I looked out just in time to see a teenage boy stealing away from our little summer chalet in the garden, heading towards the hedge at the back. He was carrying something. I ran downstairs and out of the kitchen door, and caught him halfway to the hedge. He was carrying some camera equipment we kept in the bungalow. While I kept him pinned to the ground, Cindy quickly called the police officer in the next village.

Perth came up to us on the grass. She did not growl at the boy or bare her teeth. She just looked at him sternly. I could have left him in her safekeeping, so determined was she not to let him escape.

I began to lecture the boy, who was no more than sixteen. 'You have my dog to thank for my catching you. This could be your lucky day. If you learn your lesson, my dog's vigilance today may keep you out of prison in the future. Where do you live?'

'Arundel,' he answered.

'Well, your parents won't be very happy with you.'

'Could you take your elbow off my face?' was all he said. He looked sourly at Perth.

Finally, Police Constable Apps arrived, thanked me and Perth, and took the boy away. Later, we learned that PC Apps had inspected the boy's room in Arundel and discovered a hoard of costly high-tech equipment, stolen mostly in Bury. It was all returned to its owners, a couple of whom were our delighted friends. When the word got around that Perth had been instrumental in catching the thief, for a while she became the village heroine.

That was an encouraging interlude. But Perth continued to get weaker as spring approached. She even stopped her morning expeditions. She hobbled everywhere. Her eyes were looking more haggard, her coat greyer.

Then the unimaginable happened. The children were appalled when I told them. So was Barbara.

'Barbara,' I started in trembling, 'you'll think I'm insane, and I probably am, but I've been asked to write a book about Virginian history and I need to go back there for another nine months.' I was standing in her farmyard, defenseless. She just stared at me. 'I must do this, Barbara, and I can't leave Cindy and the kids here. Cindy and I have never been parted from one another for more than three weeks.'

'But it's all right to be parted from Perth, is it? At her age and in her condition? If you leave her again, it'll kill her. I'm sure of it. She's eighteen, for heaven's sake.'

Cindy and I were weighed down with a sense of wrong-doing as we tried to convince ourselves that we must go to Virginia. Everything beautiful and stable at home taunted us, accusing us of being unfaithful, not just to Perth but also to our family life in Appletree Cottage and the village. To abandon Perth again seemed like leaving one's aged mother in a nursing home while one went off to have a great time in a foreign land. But how often did someone invite me to write a book? I was not going to Virginia for fun. And it was going to be hard work. Our village friends envied our journey, but could anyone seriously think that we relished leaving our corner of England for the New World again?

After weeks of indecision, we decided we had to go. But what would happen to Perth? To put her in Barbara's kennel now, in her state, would surely kill her, as well as bring her much suffering. The dismal fact was that she seemed not to have much longer to live anyway. It would be so cruel. And if she did survive the year, in what condition would she be when we returned home? How long would she last after that? Probably not very long. With questions like these, we inched closer every day to the inescapable, anguished conclusion that we would have to have the vet put her to sleep. The night we decided on that, I crept up to my study-garret and cried.

I could not bear to have the children know about this as it was happening, though. Or was it that I was a coward and lacked the backbone to see to it myself? Whatever the real reason, we took the problem to Barbara. I explained to her how we felt and asked her if she would take Perth to the vet once we were gone.

'No, Peter, I couldn't do it. I can see, of course, why you

think it would be a kindness to Perth to have her put down, but this is something you have to do.' I repeated that it was because of the kids that we wanted it done after they were far away. Gradually and very reluctantly, she resigned herself to the idea. 'This is not something I would do for anyone else, but I know Perth so well that I will do it. I'll clean and groom her, and then take her to the vet.'

The spring and summer passed sadly. There was a heaviness in our hearts. It began to feel like the end, the Indian summer of our lifetime with Perth. We had never seen such a beautiful English summer. The rain fell at night and the sun shone brightly by day. Everything was lush and fertile, and the long evenings were tinged with that unmatchable glowing pink twilight that one sees commonly in Britain. Cindy and I took long, slow walks with Perth in the evenings, along the river, up in the hills, along the barley and wheat fields. I carried her much of the way.

The day arrived when we had to depart. The fields had recently been harvested, leaving bare stubble, much of which was burned by the farmers to enhance the field's fertility. The dark barrenness where waving yellow grain used to be matched the brooding emptiness of our spirits. Nature seemed to us to be shrivelling and closing up.

At the very last moment, as we were driving out of the village, we stopped at the Hollow Farm Kennel. Andrew and Claire hugged Perth tearfully. I could hardly take her from them. I had told Andrew about Barbara putting Perth to sleep, so his feelings came from deep within him. Claire knew none of this, and in her innocence lamented the loss of Perth for just a while. As for Cindy, she wept openly. Claire could not understand why she broke down so completely. I quickly took Perth and carried her through the gate into Barbara's farmyard. I smelled her groggy-doggie smell for the last time. I felt her smooth ears and soft coat. I rubbed her shoulders as for eighteen years she had loved me to do. I placed my nose on her muzzle and looked deep into her eyes.

'Bye, old girl. You're the most glorious dog the world has ever seen. Thanks, dear dogge, for the life you've given us. I love you so much, dear Perth. Can you forgive me for the nasty things I've done to you? You deserved a much better master.'

She looked at me intensely, longingly. The love in her eyes reached deep down inside of me. I wet her with my tears. She licked my hand and face a couple of times. I hugged her hard and long. Then I knocked loudly on the door. Barbara appeared and I placed Perth gently in her arms. Barbara could see I was an emotional wreck and knew enough not to say anything. We just looked at each other. Perth looked at me, too. I kissed her soft brown head once more, turned quickly and walked away. There was no sound behind me from Perth as I left.

Chapter 22

I ask the reader to travel to Virginia with us, to picture us again in that distant world, to think of Perth as we did from three thousand miles away. There was heavy snow that year, so that we felt further removed than ever from our green Sussex. Cindy and I often looked at each other with the knowledge that for all but one of the twenty years of our marriage we had lived with Perth. We could not imagine the next twenty years without her. Half our lives had had Perth in it.

Christmas came and passed and the Virginia spring soon assaulted us with a spectacular display of dogwood, redbud, magnolia, apple and cherry tree blossoms. It was lovely but I was not seduced. I had done my research and was eager to return home in June. We were all aching to get back. Andrew and Claire were devastated by the news of Perth's death, but we had had eight months to get used to the idea. I sent Barbara a large, illustrated coffee-table book about dogs for Christmas. But she had not written back. She had felt the dreariness and gloom of Perth's fate and to write to us with the details was probably the last thing she wanted to do.

One day in April a letter finally arrived from her. I still have the letter so I can let Barbara speak for herself:

Dear Peter and Cindy,

My Christmas letter to you came back yesterday from the States, I suppose because I sent it to the wrong street. It was a long explanatory letter about Perth, also a letter of very many thanks for that lovely book you sent me. You must have thought it was extraordinary that I did not acknowledge it! The book is greatly prized.

Now, about Perth. When you went and left me to get the job done, each night I thought I would phone for the vet the next morning. Then one night I came to a decision, and that was that if she became ill I would call the vet – not to have her treated but to have her put to sleep – and in the meantime I would keep her free of charge for you. Since then she has never had a day's illness! And with the weather getting better she will be able to sit in the sun more.

When do you return? I feel that she will still be with us! Is that against your wish? If it is I feel that you will have to do something yourself. I just can't bring myself to do it when she is quite well. She has a heat lamp at night if ever the weather is cold; otherwise there is nothing unusual about her!

I hope that you are all well and enjoying life. Again very many thanks for the book.

Love, Barbara

The jubilation in our rented house after I read the letter out loud can be imagined. We danced around the living room. 'My gosh, my gosh, my gosh,' Cindy shouted. 'Perth is still alive!'

'It's like the Resurrection,' I chimed in. 'Perth has been reborn. She's immortal! Eternal! She's like the phoenix that rises out of the ashes of everyone else's fears and doubts. What a dog!'

Andrew understood perfectly what had happened.

'Just think,' he screamed, 'in a month we'll see her again! I can't wait to run out into the field with her.' Claire caught the spirit of the moment and jumped on everybody in excitement. But not for some time afterwards did she learn of the issues of life and death, of gloom and triumph, through which we had suffered.

'And Barbara says she's doing well, too,' Cindy added. 'To think of it, for eight months we've thought she was gone. Now, with one letter, that's been banished. It never was real. I just know she'll be with us for a long time still. And we're never going to leave her again, no matter what.'

I agreed. And this time I knew I would never leave Perth again. It could be no other way. She had survived everything.

We arrived in England in late May on a sunny, clear morning. The landscape was resplendent with the joy of the sunshine. The rambling roses were draped in profusion over walls and gates, the trees were dressed in their fresh, clean greenery, the fields were robed in emerald and the purple wisteria was hanging everywhere. Everything sparkled with the early morning dew. England had never looked so beautiful to us and it was good to be alive.

We drove into Bury in late morning, up the Hollow, and into the kennel. Our hearts were thumping wildly. Who would have thought on that depressing morning nine months ago when in despair I carried Perth towards what we thought was her last stop that we would now be returning to pick her up again. Our sad hearts were filled with a bright morning hope in the fresh spring.

Barbara had never been so thrilled to see us. We all hugged

her this time. There she stood in her large dressing gown amid her dogs in the farmyard, the angel who had brought Perth's deliverance. We thought she should be canonised. St Barbara of Hollow Farm. She walked briskly over to get Perth. In a few seconds we saw her emerge from the barn, looking so well. She may not have seen us clearly across the yard, but she ran towards us, limping slightly but still running. Her coat was clean and shiny, like the day. We met her halfway and took her up in our arms. She smelled good, so real.

Then with a goodbye to Barbara it was on to Appletree Cottage. It was wonderful to behold, the wisteria hanging from the vines on the cottage in large globes of purple, and flowers everywhere. We ran into the garden and breathed the summer air blowing in fragrances from across the fields. The views were reassuring and magical. The river below wound its way along the valley in vivid blue. Perth set herself immediately to sniffing around the whole place, her tail wagging furiously. Life was starting again for her. And for us.

Since settling in Bury we had had many idyllic English summers, but that summer was the zenith of joy. Life could be no better. We were all together, all the time. Perth continued in good health. She hobbled around still, her hearing poor and her eyesight dimmed, but she was in no pain. And she stayed well. She was nineteen that summer. Two more years she lived, reaching the human equivalent of 147 years of age. And what a life of courage, stamina, adventure, freedom and survival it had been. She had not been everyone's favourite. But she was a genius among dogs.

We buried her in the garden. There she lies today. The lawnmower runs over her, the children play above her, Cindy and I lose ourselves in the glorious views over the hedge next to her, always lowering our eyes to her permanent corner in the garden, thinking of the twenty-one years when she roamed unfettered over the earth.

I'm telling this story about Perth many years after she died. As I think back over time I see that my own youth has gone. Our children have grown up, I've taught for what seems like centuries, and now we spend half the year in Spain, half still in Appletree Cottage in our beloved West Sussex. But it is as if Perth is still with us. We talk about her all the time. Those unhappy days in Vermont still hurt me when I think of them. She was a dog larger than life, not your typical adorable pet, not the kind of dog you will find as the heroine of a book or movie. The suffering she caused us is nothing of course compared to the yoke of human misery we hear about every day all over the world, nothing compared to the private tragedies and public calamities that damage the lives of millions. But Perth nevertheless was a powerful shaper of our lives, at times causing us the profoundest agony. She also brought us enough adventure, drama, and joy to last a lifetime. She changed us forever. I often think it is one of life's incongruities that a dog like Perth can live only twenty-one years and that people like us have to live out the rest of our days without her. Our children took over from her, but of course Perth was irreplaceable. There has not been a day since her death when I have not thought of her. I am content.

> To be, contents his natural desire,
> He asks no Angel's wing, no Seraph's fire;
> But thinks, admitted to that equal sky,
> His faithful dog shall bear him company.
> (Alexander Pope)